PEACE

PEACE

AND WHERE TO FIND IT

CHRISTOPHER PAPADOPOULOS
FOREWORD BY ECKHART TOLLE

namaste
PUBLISHING

Vancouver, Canada

Library and Archives Canada Cataloguing in Publication

Papadopoulos, Christopher, 1966-
[You are peace]
    Peace : and where to find it / Christopher Papadopoulos.

Previously published under title: You are peace.
ISBN 978-1-897238-77-6 (pbk.)

1. Peace of mind. I. Title. II. Title: You are peace.

BF637.P3P37 2015   158.1   C2014-908000-X

Published in Canada by
NAMASTE PUBLISHING
P.O. Box 62084
Vancouver, British Columbia V6J 4A3
www.namastepublishing.com

Distributed in the United States and Canada by
PGW, Berkeley, California USA

Cover design by Diane McIntosh
Typesetting by Steve Amarillo / Urban Design
Back cover photo copyright © Robert Murphy

Printed and bound in Canada by Friesens

CONTENTS

ACKNOWLEDGMENTS

Although he did not see the birth of this book, my father's kindness, wisdom, and unconditional acceptance certainly made it possible. I am grateful to my mother for her love and for always welcoming me back home and taking me in, no questions asked.

My appreciation and thanks to my brothers Peter and Philip for their humor and for being a valuable mirror to look into as I have grown up and evolved.

I would like to thank Veronica Lehner and Kaleb Newsom for their feedback and encouragement early on in the writing process. I am also thankful to Suzanne Lord, Bernard Gloster, and Victoria Ritchie for their help in trying to get my words out into the world.

A special heartfelt thank you goes to the entire team at Namaste Publishing for their professionalism and kindness. I am especially indebted to Constance Kellough for her belief in this book's message and for being a loving and guiding presence throughout this publishing journey. My thanks to Lucinda Beacham for her help and attention to the smallest detail during the editing process. It has been an honor and a pleasure to work with David Robert Ord, a master editor who has transformed my words into an eminently readable book.

I would also like to thank Eckhart Tolle for his support, guidance, and being the inspiration that has peacefully hovered over this entire project.

Finally, I would like to express my deepest gratitude to Emma Pradel for the unconditional love and support that buoyed me every step of the way.

FOREWORD

If you have lived long enough, at some point the disconcerting thought may occur to you that lasting peace or happiness may forever elude you. Of course, there are moments or even periods of satisfaction, perhaps when you are engaged in some creative endeavor, or when a desire has just been fulfilled, a goal achieved, or some sensory pleasure is providing momentary satisfaction. Before long, however, a gain turns into a loss, an achievement ceases to be fulfilling or brings with it completely unforeseen new problems. Or perhaps a success in one area of your life is marred by failure in another, or after falling in love you fall out of love, which often means the very person that first made you happy, then makes you unhappy. So it seems that most of the time there is some challenge or some disruption of one kind or another happening in your life situation.

Relationships, family, work, money, health—these are the main factors that make up your life situation and most probably at this time at least one of these factors is not only problematic, but a source of suffering and unhappiness in your life. If your life situation is totally satisfying right now, just wait! Before long, something will "go wrong" again!

It was one of the great insights of the Buddha two and a half thousand years ago that all the conditions that make up human existence are in constant flux, impermanent, and inherently unstable. And this is why life is always problematic, always challenging. Sometimes the problems come at you from the outside, at other times from within, in the form of dysfunctional thinking, and you may not even realize it! You may also be faced with the challenge of having to live with the accumulated residues within you of emotional pain from the past, which I call the pain-body. It becomes obvious that the world isn't designed to make you happy!

However, there is ample evidence to support the assumption that the world is here to challenge you, since that is what it does all the time (unless the world is no more than an accidental accumulation of atoms and molecules, "a tale told by an idiot, full of sound and fury, signifying nothing"—which it isn't, although science and our mainstream culture still hold that belief). It's not only humans who get challenged here. All life forms do. All life forms are on an evolutionary journey, and they all evolve through being challenged, through encountering and then overcoming obstacles to manifesting their evolutionary potential. It is through challenges that more consciousness is generated.

Does that mean that peace is impossible in this world? Is peace even desirable, considering that we grow through being challenged and deepen through suffering?

The good news is that there is a transcendent peace, the arising of which is not the result of things going smoothly in your life. That peace is not of this world and does not depend on external conditions. The Buddha referred to it when he spoke of "the end of suffering" as a state of consciousness that is possible for humans to realize, and Jesus called it "the peace that passeth all understanding." How do we find it?

The answer to this is the subject matter of this book, but let me address the essence of it briefly here. Once you realize that the world isn't meant to make you happy, but to challenge you, it may become easier not only to recognize your habitual resistance patterns that arise when things "go wrong," but to actually let go of the underlying thought that assumes "this should not be happening to me." You may then also discover that most of your unhappiness is not caused by challenging situations, but by the thoughts that your mind is weaving around them, the story you are telling yourself about them. You will then be able to experiment with letting go of thoughts that create unhappiness in whatever form.

Here is what the Dhammapada, an ancient Buddhist scripture, has to say about it:

"He insulted me, he hurt me, he defeated me, he robbed me."

Those who think such thoughts will not be free from hate.

"He insulted me, he hurt me, he defeated me, he robbed me."

Those who think not such thoughts will be free from hate.

Hate, of course, is one of the many forms unhappiness can take. You get your first glimpses of transcendent peace whenever you refrain from imposing such dysfunctional thoughts on situations or people. When you make friends with the present moment, when you "let it be," no matter what form it takes, then whatever happens, happens against that background of "being," which is peace. You then not only emanate peace, but that peace also changes the way in which you deal with situations, any action you take, any words you speak. How you respond to a situation or person in the present moment will shape the form the next moment will take and will have endless repercussions in the future. This is the only way the world can and will change.

Once you have had some glimpses of that transcendent peace, you can invite it into your life, so to speak. Once a certain level of consciousness has been reached, peace becomes a matter of choice for you. Of course, at times you may forget you have a choice, or your ego's old reactive patterns may reassert themselves so strongly that they temporarily remove the possibility of choice. But then the light of awareness re-emerges and dispels the darkness of unconsciousness.

Inviting transcendent peace into your life necessarily implies becoming aware of yourself as Presence, the formless and timeless consciousness that underlies all thinking, feeling, and perceiving. In *The Power of Now*, I describe the simplicity of this realization, which takes no time because it is synonymous with present moment awareness. To become aware of this Presence, you need to become aware not only of the sometimes naturally occurring brief gaps between thoughts, but create more and longer gaps of "no thought" in the otherwise incessant stream of involuntary thinking.

If you have read *The Power of Now*, you will be familiar with the concept of "inner body awareness" and, more importantly, the practice of it. It is a powerful and easy way of stepping out of the stream of compulsive thinking and connecting with the essence of who you are. It is only when you know who you are that you can be at peace and thus no longer resent or be devastated by the challenges of life when they arise.

PEACE takes you more deeply into the practice of inner body awareness until it ceases to be a practice and becomes a way of being. The words that make up this book clearly emerged out of the state of Presence and thus have the transformational power that is a characteristic of such books.

Readers who are already familiar with *The Power of Now,* and responded to it deeply, will derive the greatest benefit from *PEACE.* Its main message is that peace is possible, even in the midst of turmoil. It is possible because it is inseparable from who you are in your essence.

ECKHART TOLLE, *Author*

The Power of Now
A New Earth
Stillness Speaks

DEDICATION

For my father
1939 - 2007

THE SEARCH FOR PEACE

One morning in the fall of 2003, I walked into the kitchen and remarked to my mother, "You know what? I'm not seeking anymore."

A peace-infused clarity had moved from the background to the foreground of my awareness. Suddenly, feeling peaceful seemed quite normal. Other than my memories of a life lived mostly lost in thought or reacting to things emotionally, it felt as though peace had always been my natural state.

It was as if I had come home to myself.

Only now did I notice how deeply embedded the "seeking" me had been. I had no idea of the extent of my anxiety, and how desperately I had wanted to find peace, until after years of seeking, that morning my distress was finally gone for good.

Everyone wants to feel peaceful, don't they? People go out of their way to avoid stressful situations, or to bring about their dreams, in the hope of finding peace.

Would it surprise you if I told you that feeling peaceful has nothing to do with your current personal *situation,* but everything to do with *where your attention is?*

To illustrate what I'm talking about, if you are in a room right now, are there more things in this room, or is there more space? You may not have noticed until now, but there's far more space in most rooms than there are things. The average room is, in fact, mostly space. Indeed, the world itself is mostly empty space—atmosphere, with shapes on the ground. Isn't this also true of the universe itself?

The apparent solidity of anything material is a perceptual illusion.

Even the atoms that make up matter are almost completely empty space, since the nucleus and electrons constitute an infinitesimal part of the atom. The space between individual atoms is even greater, regardless of the material. We could lift the roof off a house and pour concrete until every inch from bottom to top is filled, but the resulting solid block would still be more than 99.99 % empty space.

Did all of this space just arrive, or was it here long before us? Of course, it's been here a very long time. We just weren't aware of it.

Where should I be looking for peace?

You may think you've looked *everywhere* for peace. You may feel quite frustrated, perhaps even exasperated, because you believe you've looked everywhere, tried everything, and come up empty. However, I've already shown you there is a reality around you that you likely haven't paid attention to before now. You may not have even noticed this at all.

The fact you've looked in so many places for peace and not found it is actually good news. Even though you believe you've looked everywhere, you have just experienced how easy it is not to notice something that's in fact very, very obvious. Just as you didn't really notice how empty everything is, so too you haven't noticed that the peace you crave is actually *right here already*.

In fact, the peace you have been looking for emanates from the emptiness of the space we've just been talking about, the space in which you exist. Peace has always been here, and indeed everywhere, without us knowing it. Once you learn how to tune into the peace that's already here, you'll have all the peace you could wish for. If you aren't at peace with yourself, you certainly haven't looked right where you are. How do I know this? Because to look here, you have to *be* here.

What do I mean by "be here"?

To be here, you have to be in the present moment, giving it your full attention. Sadly, instead of being here, in most cases our minds are elsewhere.

When we aren't completely here in this moment now, we don't experience reality as it actually is. Instead, we view it through a heavy filter of beliefs, thoughts, and emotions. These are characteristics of the mind, which we might think of as an interpreting and measuring mechanism. If you pay attention to your thoughts, you'll notice they are constantly evaluating everything, commenting on everything, drawing conclusions about everything.

The problem is, the constant interpreting and evaluating that takes place when the mind is active tends to disconnect us from the aliveness of reality. In other words, the thoughts we use to try to understand reality have a way of removing us from the actual experience of reality.

Let's focus on thought for a moment. Are you aware there's an almost constant monologue going on in your head? There is, though many of us aren't aware of it unless we actually stop and pay attention to our thoughts.

This "voice in the head"[1] carries on a conversation with itself during most of our waking hours. It's as if we're talking to ourselves all the time. But this voice isn't our own—isn't the voice of our true self. It's a foreign voice.

Even if, unlike most people, you're aware of this voice in your head, you may never have thought of it as a foreign voice. Because you're so completely identified with it, it just sounds like your own thoughts. Until you step back from them, that is, and suddenly become aware that all of these thoughts and various emotions are arising without you doing anything to cause them. They aren't you at all! They are just something happening inside your head, and you are the one listening to them, noticing them, observing them.

It might help to think of the voice in your head as software that's been programmed into you and is now running on your hardwiring, the neural circuits of your brain. This software goes under various brand

[1] Tolle, Eckhart. *A New Earth*, Dutton, 2005, p. 30.

names. The one I like to use was coined by Eckhart Tolle in his book *The Power of Now*. He calls this software the "ego."

Are you saying that my ego is different from who I really am?

Ego is a term that's been around for thousands of years. But over the centuries, it's meaning has changed. It has been used to refer to everything from our authentic self to a false sense of self, and even to specific aspects of ourselves such as in the way Freud used it. Different people use the term ego to mean different things.

When I speak of ego, I'm referring not to who we *really* are, but to a false sense of ourselves—an idea of ourselves, an image of ourselves, a picture of ourselves we carry around in our head.

You can see what I mean if someone says to you, "I need to improve my self-image." There's an observer who sees the image and concludes it needs improving. Or someone might say something like, "I don't see myself that way." Their interpretation of how they come across is different from your sense of how they come across.

As mentioned, the software that's almost constantly running on our neural circuits drops a heavy filter of beliefs, thoughts, and emotions over reality. This conceptual filter goes largely unnoticed. It's so subtle, it remains superimposed on our perception of reality for most of our lives unless something awakens us to its presence. The result is that the mental processes associated with this software consume most of our attention, leaving little room for seeing the way things *really* are—including who *we* really are.

Most humans suffer from a case of mistaken identity. We believe ourselves to be our thoughts, emotions, and behavior, each of which are products of the mind. We think of ourselves as "me" with a story about our likes, dislikes, what happened to us in the past, and what we want to happen in the future. In fact, we often associate life with "what's happening to us."

If you pay close attention, you'll see that all of our thoughts, emotions, and behavior—along with all the things that are happening to us—occur on the *surface* of reality. Hidden behind the scenes is a silent, invisible intelligence that observes these things. This invisible intelligence is pure awareness. It has no shape or form, but simply *is*. We might think of it as pure "being," that which exists before actual things and events come into being. In other words, it's the *source* of all shapes, forms, and everything that happens. It's where objects, nature, people, places, events, thoughts, and emotions originate.

This pure being—this intelligence from which everything has arisen—can't be known through words or concepts. It's impossible to describe it, or even imagine it. Instead, it has to be *experienced*.

I liken it to a grapefruit. If you had never seen a piece of fruit of any kind, and I began describing a grapefruit to you, no matter how hard I might try, you would have little idea of what a grapefruit is. The only way you could know what I'm talking about would be to see a grapefruit, hold it, peel it, taste it, and swallow it. In other words, it must be experienced to be known. In effect, only when we become one with the grapefruit, so that we absorb its nutrients, do we really grasp what it is.

In our essential being, each of us is pure awareness. So as long as we identify ourselves with the voice in our head, we are living with a case of mistaken identity. To be identified with the content of our mind is to inhabit a virtual world, which in effect means we live in the abstract realm of thought.

To discover who we really are, we must step back from the thinker that pretends to be us, including the images we hold of ourselves. We must look beneath our mental clutter to find its source, which is the spaciousness of pure awareness. Only then can we detect this ever-present awareness as our true nature, which is pure *being*. Let me be clear what I mean when I speak of pure awareness. When we say, "I'm aware of the situation," we are indicating that we are cognizant of our thoughts *about* a situation. This is the way we typically describe awareness. But behind our mental content, our body, and the universe, there is an eternally awake, present, and formless source of everything that exists. This pure awareness has always been and will forever be. This is who we truly are.

When we refocus our attention to become aware of awareness

itself, we don't identify with any thought, emotion, object, or event. We are not being "this" or "that." As an expression of the awareness that precedes the emergence of all shapes and forms, we are simply *being*. We are one with the source of, and the silent witness to, all that can be perceived and conceived.

I hear so many people say it's important to "be here now." Why?

We've all heard expressions such as "be here now," "be in the moment," "stay in the now," "just live in the present moment." So when I talk about pure "being," you're likely saying to yourself, "Haven't we heard all of this before?"

Yes, millions have heard about the need to live in the present moment. Yet here we are, most of us still struggling, hurting, year after year. Obviously it's not enough that we hear about living in the moment, and that everyone from sports figures to movie stars talk about it these days, or people wouldn't be suffering as they are. It has to become an actual experience that we no longer talk about or even try to do. It has to be experienced as our state of *being*.

Sometimes people feel they've had enough of all this talk about the present moment. They believe they know about the present moment, since they've read a lot of books and been to many retreats to deepen their understanding of the subject. After sometimes years trying to be in the present, they're tired of it all.

The actual present moment is never fatiguing or irritating. Quite the opposite, it's the very definition of vibrancy, joy, clarity, and peace. The beautiful mystery of the present fills you with wonder as you experience relief and liberation.

What you have "had enough of " is the *concept* of the present moment, which teases you with its hopeful possibilities but always remains just out of reach. Whenever you feel this way, it's because your mind is forcing itself up against reality, trying to extract an understanding of it through mental interpretation alone. In this way, your mind acts as an invisible barrier between you and reality. Like two magnets whose like poles are facing each other, whatever you reach out for, whatever you seek to understand, is actually pushed further away by the very act of trying to grasp it mentally.

The wonderful thing is that life is hardwired to bring us experiences that invite us to step into the present moment. In fact, life will keep on bringing us such experiences, repeating the message about living in the moment as it were, until everyone begins to embody what the words point to.

When we make the shift into just being in the present, we experience a deep, vibrant peace that's vast and intelligent—a peace that's nothing to do with how we might attempt to rearrange our lives or alter what's happening to us in the hope of making things more peaceful for ourselves.

We discover peace as our primordial characteristic, which has always been there.

You seem to be suggesting that people have a misconception of what peace is.

In his huge hit *Imagine*, John Lennon sings the words, "Imagine all the people living life in peace." It's a wonderful image.

However, the word "peace" poses an interesting challenge. It's been used in so many different ways that it's lost much of its meaning. Reduced to platitudes in endless speeches and a symbol on t-shirts and bumper stickers, it's little more than an idea in people's heads—an idea that's different for different people.

Consider some of the ways people imagine what it would be like for everyone to live in peace. For a Muslim, Christian, or Jew of a fundamentalist persuasion, it could be that the only way there could ever be peace on earth would be for everyone to adhere to the identical beliefs and same strict practices they themselves embrace. For many of them, strict adherence to Islamic law, a literal interpretation of the Bible, or rigorous practice of Torah are essential for there to be peace. In contrast, for someone who doesn't believe in any kind of God, for everyone to "do their own thing," as long as they don't hurt another person, would be a state of peace. No one would control anyone.

The world is plagued with violence and untold cruelty. For many, peace means simply an absence of violence—an end to cruelty, torture, abuse, and especially war. For them, the world would be at peace if nations and individuals were no longer caught up in conflict with one another.

I suggest our concepts of peace, which inevitably conflict with other people's, fail to point us in the direction of real peace. In fact, they take us in the opposite direction because they lead us to imagine peace is something that can be found externally—by practicing a strict code, pursuing whatever lifestyle we prefer, or simply not engaging in fighting.

I can see how none of this brings people a deep sense of calm, contentment, and joy. People don't feel at peace within themselves.

A growing number of people are realizing they long for something more than a pseudo peace that's only surface deep. They want the kind of peace that soothes their nerves, quiets their anxiety, and stills their emotional turmoil. Consequently, many are attracted to the kind of philosophy espoused by influential author and inspirational speaker Dale Carnegie, who stated, "Nothing can bring you peace but yourself."

Carnegie was of course correct. Only we can experience peace—it isn't something someone else can bequeath to us. Yet even this concept can take us away from real peace if we imagine peace as something we have to "work at."

Unfortunately, the more deeply we are enmeshed in the conceptual realm, the more cliché and meaningless the words of people like John Lennon and Dale Carnegie become. Cut off from our true selves, we mistake the reality of peace for some abstract ideal. This is what the mind, the conceptualizer, does to all of reality. It shifts our attention from the actual experience of something and creates a virtual copy in the head for us to look at and identify with. The longer we remain transfixed by the images and thoughts in our head, the further we move away from the reality we wish to experience.

My sense is that John Lennon and Dale Carnegie ultimately had in mind a deeper truth than how their words are frequently understood. They no doubt caught a glimpse of the peace that's inherent in *being* itself.

A common term for the phenomenon Carnegie referred to is "inner peace." However, it's important to recognize that "inner" doesn't mean "inside." Rather, it refers to the inner dimension of formlessness—the primordial substrate from which all the shapes and forms that make up the world emerge.

It's time to liberate peace from the prison of the mind, the abstract realm. The key to this is to realize that the peace we long for is the living, breathing reality of who we truly are. It can never be understood conceptually, since it possesses a depth and permanence far beyond the superficial and temporary calmness that's typically referred to as peace.

This book will show you how to live from your true nature, which is always peaceful. It's your birthright to experience peace as a constant background to everything that happens in your life. In a sense, this is a roadmap home, back to your true self. By going in the direction this book points, you'll enter into your own direct experience of being at home with yourself. You will be the evidence that peace is available right now, no matter what may be happening in your external world. The implications of such a discovery literally constitute an evolutionary leap in consciousness.

Is personal peace in some way related to peace on the planet?

Yes—and in fact we will never experience planetary peace without going deep into this moment to experience the source of all peace. Most of humanity have been looking for peace in the wrong place for thousands of years.

Throughout history, there has never been a time when humans brought about peace. What was claimed to be peace was just superficial and temporary. A cease-fire between two warring nations is only a declaration of less violence for a limited period—a promise to refrain from behavior the ego finds irresistible. This isn't peace.

Although a temporary calm is certainly preferable to violence and upset, it disappears soon after it arrives because the ego—the image of ourselves we carry around in our head—is by nature dissatisfied, and its compulsive thinking and reactivity makes it prone to new rounds of negativity. Consequently, just as nations haven't been able to bring about peace in the past through wars, negotiations, and treaties, so too all future attempts to create peace are destined to fail.

Peace isn't two leaders shaking hands in front of flashing cameras and to loud applause.

Peace isn't a ceremony in which documents are signed at a table.

Peace isn't a panoramic view of a sleepy town below.

Peace isn't an afternoon in bed reading, a morning in the basement repairing a chair, or an evening watching television.

Peace isn't someone holding two fingers outwards in a V for victory sign.

This list could become quite long if we tried to think of all the scenarios that depict calmness, inactivity, or symbolic behavior. But none of these are what I mean when I speak of peace.

So a quiet town isn't necessarily evidence of a deep or lasting serenity?

No, because behind each door of a seemingly quiet town live one or more egos, which inevitably create suffering for themselves and often each other. Leisurely behavior or a quiet mood is subject to change at short notice. Neither does it reflect the tension, distraction, and unease that lie below the surface. These are at best temporary states of calm.

While we are busy trying to forge, broker, negotiate, establish, or in some other way create what can't be created, we miss the peace that's already here. Peace is permanent and is present behind the scenes in each and every situation, waiting to be recognized and experienced. Peace should never be confused with symbols, ceremonies, or other activities. All thoughts, intentions, emotions, objects, and events are impermanent. They are constantly shifting and changing, growing or dissolving, whereas peace has always been here and always will be here.

The good news is that once we cease resisting this reality, the personal and planetary peace we have struggled and longed for will appear. This is because the peace we long for to end our personal distress is the same peace nations seek—a peace that's now fast becoming essential for the survival of our species. Personal and planetary peace are related because our longing for peace is, at the deepest level, our desire to discover who we truly are. Each step an individual takes toward discovering themselves has them moving closer to peace.

How exactly can personal peace lead to world peace?

The awakening of one person to their true nature acts as a catalyst for others. It's as if the peace emanating from that one person begins to resonate with and awaken something deep within another. As we wake up out of our false images of ourselves, we act as mirrors for those around us, so that it becomes harder for them to continue playing their roles when they encounter an authentic being. Awareness of our true self then spreads across the planet and is carried on a wave of peace.

In other words, the unseen peace that pervades the universe only becomes what we call "world peace" when the personal experience of peace becomes *widely* recognized and embodied.

You could say that peace is rather like a single living entity that engulfs and penetrates not only our entire planet, but all the galaxies, indeed the whole universe. It extends from the vastness of space to the infinitely small at the subatomic level. This living entity is the intelligence, the awareness, the essence of who each of us truly is. All we have to do is tune into it.

The search for inner peace has always been a search for who we are in our essential selves, and the quest for world peace has always been a movement toward a global awakening to our collective oneness as an expression of *being* itself. The destination, so to speak, is the same for the individual and the planet—the recognition that, deeper than all our ideas about ourselves, we are pure awareness, which is a state of vibrant peace.

Does the peace you speak of ever leave you?

Back to the kitchen where we began this journey together. When I told my mother I was no longer seeking, I noticed that her eyes focused elsewhere. Of course, she replied approvingly, "Okay, Chris, that's good." Although she was genuinely happy for me, she didn't really understand what "no longer seeking" meant.

I was more than happy. I was serene, content, and quietly amazed by what had happened.

Since that day, this peace has been with me continuously. It's accompanied by a sense that when I observe the world, I'm observing something sacred. I can feel that people, places, objects, and indeed the whole of nature are grounded in a deep sacredness. Even on the most challenging days, I feel the presence of peace somewhere beneath the tumult. I find myself aligned with something that lies beyond my wants, fears, and the stories I tell myself about life. It's as if someone turned down the volume of what's happening not only around me, but also in my own head.

Like a compass that always aligns with true north, my inner being is in permanent alignment with a peace that's both intelligent and vibrant. Even after that morning when I walked into my mother's kitchen, my experience of peace continued to grow slowly and gently, as it does to this day.

I realize that what's been happening to me for some time is something that can happen to anyone. This is encouraging, because like so many other people, I always wanted to make the world a better place. Now I know this begins with the discovery of our peaceful self.

2

AWARENESS IS THE KEY

During the annual Montreal jazz festival that happens in the summer, I came across a group of people who had gathered in front of a boutique store. Only one item was on display in the window, which was particularly noticeable because it was dusk and a spotlight fell directly on the item. It was a T-shirt, and it sported a silkscreen print of a ripe banana.

Beneath the print were the words, "This is not a banana."

The small crowd who had gathered at the window were trying to figure out what this meant, since it didn't seem to make sense. Was the banana maybe a fruit similar to a banana, such as a plantain? Was the banana somehow symbolic, perhaps conveying a hidden message? Or maybe the artist was being ironic?

No one considered the simple answer—that it wasn't an actual banana, but a T-shirt with a colorful image of a banana on it. It was a representation of a banana, but not the reality.

Now think of the word "breathing." How would you define breathing? How would you describe it? For instance, what does it look like, sound like, feel like?

Whatever images or thoughts you have about breathing, drop them for a moment and simply move fully into an awareness of your body. Feel the movement of air in your nostrils, throat, and lungs. Notice that the air you inhale has a different temperature from the air you exhale. Feel the gentle expansion and contraction of your torso with each breath.

Thinking about breathing, trying to describe it, really doesn't do much for you—except possibly engender a measure of anxiety. Yet if you continue to allow yourself to actually experience the sensation of breathing, you'll eventually feel a peacefulness wash over you.

Notice the difference between your thoughts *about* breathing and the direct felt *experience* of breathing. For most of us, so much time is spent in the virtual world of our thoughts *about* our experiences that we begin to confuse the thoughts with the experiences themselves.

In a similar way, what most people think of as peace is just an abstract concept. It's what they imagine peace to be like. But this is far from the actual experience of peace. In fact, the mind's virtual images of peace are nothing like the reality, because the ego—the false idea we all have of ourselves—blocks our direct awareness of peace.

I can remember peaceful moments from my past. Is this what you mean by peace?

We've no doubt all had peaceful moments. But when these moments came, they weren't something we brought about by *thinking* of peace.

Over time, memories we have of times when we felt tranquil get replaced by stereotypical scenarios that are meant to represent peace. This happens because a particular experience of peace isn't something we can hold onto, as if it were a "thing." Actual peace isn't an event, thought, or emotion. Instead, it's an underlying characteristic of who we *are*.

Because it's characteristic of who we are, peace never leaves us. At those times when peace appears to leave us, it's we who have abandoned peace by turning our attention away from the present moment. We lack peace because most of the time we don't even realize we've done this.

When a couple get into a heated argument, it indicates a lack of awareness of their true being. The peace that's characteristic of who they really are hasn't been destroyed at such moments, but simply veiled by their egoic thoughts and emotions.

In an active war zone, filled with gunfire, tank battles, and exploding bombs, there's so much fear and rage that the subtleness of peace becomes obscured—though it's still there. The key is to tune into ever-present peace, then observe what happens to your perception of the situation—and sometimes to the actual conflict itself.

Once you experience peace as your bedrock state, you may not look at news footage of violence in the same way. Instead of generating a sense of hopelessness and despair, you'll find it reassuring that, since peace is so very close to us even in our darkest moments, our situation on this planet is actually quite hopeful.

That said, some situations may make you feel more peaceful than others. When you see a sleeping baby or walk through a silent forest, you may feel the sheer depth of the peace that's present. Even the thought of it may make you feel a little better. But while thinking about inherently peaceful situations may produce a brief sense of wellbeing, this can never compare to the power of actual peace.

More importantly, it isn't the baby or the forest that produce peace, but their surrendered nature and lack of resistance to life. These make the peace that's already present more visible—as if the form has become translucent, revealing the formless reality beneath. We appreciate such moments because they resonate with our own deepest being.

A sleeping baby emanates peacefulness because its little body has only recently been animated. Since the ability to think is as yet undeveloped, the baby possesses no "voice in the head" to mistakenly identify with. Life can fully express itself as a peace-infused awareness, unencumbered by a false personal identity—the ego. The baby appears to be surrendered to what *is*, aligned with the "flow of life."[2] Even when the baby wakes up startled or hungry, it does so against a backdrop of peace. It's just not as easily perceived when the baby is upset.

Like a sleeping baby or a forest, the whole of nature allows peace to shine through because there's no resistance to the flow of life—to what

[2] Tolle, Eckhart. *The Power of Now,* Namaste Publishing, 1997, p. 173.

is. Nature fully inhabits the present moment, reality itself, because it exists at a level of consciousness that doesn't involve thought.

Thought pulls our species out of reality—out of the present moment—which often produces resistance to what *is*. It's this inability to leave life alone that disrupts our awareness of peace.

You mentioned resistance to the flow of life. How exactly am I resisting this flow?

By thinking about your life.

From our perspective, life is "what's happening," the seemingly endless cycle of growth and dissolution that everything undergoes. But life is also the underlying intelligence of the universe that's responsible for the creation of everything from molecules to mountains, grass to galaxies.[3]

This intelligent awareness saturates every atom, every cell, and every inch of space. As the animating force of everything that exists, it's the source of all activity, all endeavor. Whereas our minds are incapable of producing anything more than an incomplete and often distorted picture of reality, pure awareness perceives things the way they truly are.

Imagine yourself floating down the river of life. Now picture yourself standing up in the flow to get a better view of where you are. When you do so, you are no longer flowing with life. As you remain standing in the water, a feeling of pressure and unease builds in your body. It's a stressful state to be in, not at all peaceful. Similarly, the common act of thinking impedes our awareness of the flow of life and causes us distress.

Most of us believe we need to think about our lives, reflecting, analyzing, and interpreting what's happened, what's happening, and what might happen further on. This is how we chart our way through life. However, whenever we step out of the flow of life by trying to figure out where we should go next, we don't realize we're doing so from a

---

[3] Tolle, Eckhart. *Stillness Speaks*, Namaste Publishing, pp. 7-8.

stationary point of view that can't possibly know what lies around the next bend.

Prolonged resistance to the flow of life results in emotional and physical suffering. This suffering is life's way of telling us to turn our attention away from the abstract realm of thought and realign ourselves with the uninterpreted reality of the flow of life. The primordial intelligence that not only formed us, but that *is* the flow, knows how to navigate toward our fullest expression.

Thinking about our lives, trying to figure things out, is generally considered to be a good thing, a sign of being highly evolved.

Yes. But if highly evolved *is* as highly evolved *does*, the rate at which we humans are destroying ourselves and our planet doesn't speak well for how evolved we are. We think a lot, and even have "think tanks," but we don't seem to have much awareness of the consequences of our thoughts and the actions that follow from them.

It's not that analyzing something, seeking to understand it, is a problem in itself. A problem only arises when we turn our reflections, analysis, interpretations, and conclusions into an identity—an image of ourselves we feel we need to confirm or live up to.

You've heard expressions such as "get real," "keep it real," and "get a life." But have you ever stopped to realize what such expressions actually tell us about ourselves? They each relate to how thinking about our lives takes us out of the flow of life. They point to how we often say "no" to reality, substituting thought for awareness.

The misconception in a statement like "get a life" is that life is something we need to get, when it's what we *are*. How can you "get a life" when you already are life itself? As for keeping it real, it's the voice in the head that tells us to keep it real that's preventing us from experiencing reality! No one can ever get real by exhorting themselves to get real.

What we can do is relax into life, relax into reality, allowing what *arises* simply to be. When we do so, the peace that's characteristic of awareness floods our entire being. As this happens, we shift into an experience of greater awareness that we might think of as a higher state of consciousness.

Just as humans enjoy a more intense experience of consciousness than our cousins the great apes, so also there are gradations of consciousness within our species. Some people show little awareness of themselves or the events around them, whereas others exhibit considerably greater awareness. However, whatever our level of awareness, it's only a partial experience of the divine consciousness—the universal intelligence—of which everything is a manifestation.

As a species, we're right now seeking to evolve beyond our proclivity for turning our thoughts into an identity. Whenever we make thoughts an identity, it blinds us to the divine consciousness that's our essence. The evolutionary process is drawing us away from human reasoning into pure awareness, a peaceful and harmonious state in which we flow with the great river of consciousness.

The quest for personal and global peace we are witnessing in our time is a reflection of this evolution of human consciousness that's currently taking place. As a species, we're inching our way from identification with our thoughts to the realization we are the peace-infused awareness that's the source of all the shapes and forms that make up our everyday experience.

Are you saying I should never think about the things that have happened to me?

There's nothing wrong with remembering our past. The mistake is to turn any event from our past or present into an identity. The same is true of our dreams for the future. Dream, but don't make it your identity.

To illustrate what I mean, how often have you been in a coffee shop, at a party, or in an office setting, when someone initiated a conversation by saying, "Tell me about yourself."

In such a conversation, among the things you might talk about are things that have happened to you in the past, your educational background, your religious and philosophical beliefs, and your plans for the future. Yet no matter how much you reveal, you still wouldn't have told the inquirer about *yourself.*

In any conversation of this kind, out of the billions of events that have occurred in our lives, we select a mere handful of incidents and use them to paint a portrait of ourselves for the listener. If you think of life as a reel of film containing billions of frames, the story we each tell of ourselves consists of just a tiny number of clips, woven together to form a personal narrative. In other words, a few dozen people or events that had a positive or negative impact on us, along with a small selection of ideas to which our culture has exposed us, substitute for the long chronicle of reality that has actually been our experience.

Add to this the fact that even the limited number of items we select to tell what we think of as "our story" don't represent a complete picture of reality, but have themselves been given an interpretive twist to suit the image we wish to project of ourselves. For instance, when an event happens, we see it from a particular perspective and remember it a certain way. Others present at the event may experience it quite differently, if only because they are seeing it from a different angle. Each individual who witnesses the event interprets and reacts to it based on the unique way their mind has been conditioned. Since each of us is running different software—different beliefs and ideas about ourselves and our lives—we can't help but see patterns others don't see and filter reality in a way only we are capable of.

You can see how this works if you consider how your own beliefs have changed over time. Given a lifetime, our beliefs can alter drastically, sometimes constituting a complete reversal. Which past events do you use now to define yourself, in contrast to the ideas you held twenty, thirty, or forty years ago?

The defining events and cherished beliefs we use to compose a sense of "self" are no more than a narrow selection of memory traces and thoughts to which we are attached.[4] They work in concert to rein-

---

[4] Nader, Karim. "Memory Traces Unbound," Trends In Neurosciences, Volume 26, Issue 2, February 1, 2003, pp. 65-72.

force a false sense of ourselves based on ever-changing content, so that what happens to us shapes what we believe, and what we believe affects how we interpret what happens to us.

Are you telling me my whole life could be a lie?

The way we *interpret* life could perhaps be said to be a lie to some degree. More precisely, it's distorted and incomplete.

The experience of "what happened to me" is not only distorted by our mental filter during the actual event, but is further distorted during the process of consolidating our memories. There's a period of hours or days after an event when memories are in a malleable state and can be altered. Often how we remember something is influenced not only by our own judgments and reactions after the fact, but also by other people's interpretations.

But it's even more complicated than that. It used to be believed that once events were stored in long-term memory, they were no longer prone to significant alteration. However, we now know the brain goes through the unstable phase of the memory consolidation process every time we bring up a memory. In other words, it appears that the act of pulling up a memory to be reviewed once again exposes it to that malleable stage in which it's prone to alteration, and this can happen again and again.[5]

When we create an identity out of certain memories, it means we are constantly pulling them out of long-term memory and exposing them to the particular beliefs and reactive patterns of our current situation. This means our mental filter can distort the very memories that comprise our identity. Since our beliefs and emotional reactions change over the years, it's likely the memories on which we've based our identity have little to do with the original events that occurred years ago.

Given memory malleability and the fact human behavior is largely controlled by a dysfunctional ego, what does an event really teach us about who we truly are?

---

[5] Ibid.

Are you saying that my life story isn't important?

The "story of me" we all tell ourselves isn't necessary, and in fact impedes our awareness of many wonderful qualities of our essential being, such as love, joy, beauty, wonder, creativity, and peace. The superficial and changing details of our lives—the who, what, where, and so on—are much less important than these eternal qualities, since these are what make life truly worth living.

A shift in consciousness—away from thought to awareness—shines a light on the events of our lives, revealing how our attempts to "make memories" in order to make our lives meaningful are a substitute for what we really seek, which is the essential qualities of our deeper being.

There comes a point when we experience such a shift from our previous understanding of ourselves that it's often referred to as a "spiritual awakening" or "enlightenment." This isn't a religious experience, although it can occur in the context of one's faith. As this shift to a much higher level of awareness takes hold, we find ourselves increasingly understanding our mind and body as but an expression of our deeper being. Consequently, we no longer identify with our thoughts and fluctuating emotions, but with the deeper states characteristic of our being—love, joy, and peace.

Simultaneously, we recognize that the present moment is all there ever is. The past and future are mere mental abstractions. Fully present in this moment now, we experience peace, fulfillment, clarity, a gentle joy, and great relief that we don't have to carry around our burdensome personal history anymore. As previously mentioned, even during the most difficult days, we are reassured by the presence of deep peace in the background.

Can you imagine what a difference such a shift makes in the life of someone who has suffered greatly from an event in the past?

For instance, a tragic form of abuse that seems to repeatedly make headlines these days concerns the number of people of both sexes who have fallen prey to sexual predators. The abuse by priests, parents, or other authority figures seems a particularly horrendous betrayal of trust. As devastating as such cases of abuse are, what makes them even more tragic is the way our culture teaches us to turn them into an identity. The fact that a person was abused, whether for a brief moment or over a period of years, now comes to define them, seemingly forever destroying the quality of their life.

When an abused individual recognizes that the things that have happened to them, and how they've been tortured by the memory of such events, has nothing to do with their essential being, the relief they experience is immense. They have the opportunity to realize that who they really are has never, ever been abused, and this realization can bring them into an awareness of the peace that has never left them—a peace that it may even be possible to enter into while the abuse is actually going on if a person is very present. To be present in this way, aware that this isn't happening to one's true self, is entirely different from dissociating under the impact of trauma.

From here on, such individuals no longer think of themselves as victims—no longer define themselves by what happened to them, often long ago.

So the emotional pain I've been feeling all these years is unnecessary?

When great suffering involves the violation and abuse of the physical body, it's one of the greatest challenges a human being can face. No one wishes to lessen what you've gone through. It was clearly terrible, perhaps unbearable. And yet, it's also true that we don't have to suffer our whole life long when something of this kind happens to us.

However, even as I tell you that all such suffering is unnecessary, I sense something in you may not like hearing that the pain you've experienced doesn't need to become a lifelong burden. It could be that a part of you actually identifies with being a victim. This is not uncommon. If this is the case, it's important to understand what your resistance to feeling the peace and joy that's your true self is about.

I credit Eckhart Tolle's book *The Power of Now* for being the catalyst in my own awakening and awareness of many things, including a sub-personality that Eckhart calls "the pain-body."[6]

The pain-body is the reason many of us, to one degree or another, are attracted to the idea we are "wounded," "abused," or "victims," sometimes wearing such an identity as if it were a badge of honor. This sub-personality of unreleased pain from our past includes patterns of behavior we're often unconscious of but that draw us into situations that generate even more pain.

When emotional pain isn't fully observed, accepted, and released, it doesn't go away. On the contrary, it accumulates, eventually becoming a mass of pain. Like our unobserved thoughts, our unobserved emotions become part of our identity. Strong negative emotions then live on in the energy field of the body as a semiautonomous entity, the "pain-body." We might think of it as an alter ego.

If you've ever heard someone say, "He's beside himself with anger," it's this semiautonomous entity—this alter ego—that's being referred to. The person is so overcome with anger that it's as if another person has emerged that isn't truly who we know the person to be.

We're pointing to the same phenomenon when we say a person "isn't herself today." The individual is so consumed with sadness, anxiety, or some other disquieting emotion that's preoccupying them, they appear almost to be a different person. In other words, the pain-body's power comes from being an unobserved phenomenon that takes us over without our knowing it. Afterwards, we may well be shocked by what we said or did while we were "losing it" and feel a need to apologize deeply or even make amends.

When we feel a dark mood wash over us, or a heaviness descend on us, this too is the pain-body. It can also hide in everyday negativity such as impatience, resentment, guilt, and sadness. The negative emotion is often accompanied by "should"-filled thoughts, as we tell ourselves, "That should never have happened" or, "This isn't supposed to be happening." In essence, we're saying "no" to reality. Of course, resisting what *is* only generates further anguish.

Just as the "thinker" in us requires more thought in order to

---

[6] Tolle, Eckhart. *The Power of Now*, Namaste Publishing, 1997, p. 29.

survive, the pain-body requires more pain for its continued existence. It *needs* to feel hurt, and typically emerges from time to time to feast on negativity, especially drama. At such a moment, the details of a situation can seem terribly important, engendering argument and even rupturing relationships. However, the feeling of urgency or "rightness" we experience at such times is simply the pain-body merging with our thoughts to produce more pain to feed on in order to perpetuate itself. Notice how the details of "who did what" are much less important when the pain-body recedes—not because the situation has changed, which it may not have, but because the pain-body's appetite for negative energy has been temporarily satisfied.

Whenever we are taken over by the pain-body, we are in a sense reliving our wounded past. Constrained by this heavy filter, we're incapable of perceiving ourselves or others clearly. In this deeply altered state, we actually crave negativity and take a kind of pleasure in more suffering. Once the pain-body's store of negativity has been replenished, it returns to a dormant state, awaiting the next opportunity to feel offended or victimized so it can feed again and thereby perpetuate itself.

Once the deeply unaware state of the pain-body passes, we generally return to our normal level of functioning—although in some people the suffering and dysfunction is so chronic that the pain-body remains active most of the time. You can see this in the person who is sad much of the time, continually anxious, or a rageaholic.

Can we ever get rid of this pain from our past?

The good news is that the pain-body can be dissolved in the same way as any other aspect of our false persona.

Whatever thoughts or emotions arise, the way forward is to completely allow them to be as they are. Becoming very alert, we give them our full attention without either reacting to or interpreting what's happening. The key is to bring our awareness to the sensations of pressure, urgency, or "rightness" we are experiencing, without giving voice to the victim story the ego provides to accompany these sensations. Attending to the physical sensations quiets our thoughts and calms our emotions, returning us to the present moment.

There's another reason negativity comes seemingly out of nowhere to drop a distorting mood over our perceptions. Since at the deepest level we are all interconnected, it follows that there's a collective energy field of pain.[7] As a species, a nationality, a particular gender, race, or family, we possess a group pain-body. The cruelty, abuse, and atrocities a group has faced remain in each member's energy field as a background of pain. As, one by one, we become aware of this collective pain, the peace that's part of our true nature begins to replace the layer of pain of the various subgroups with which we identify.

The pain-body can't survive in the light of our awareness. Consequently, each time we bring our awareness to it, we dissolve a little more of our painful past, until its residue has gone completely.

Having said all this, you can take comfort in the fact that when the egoic "me" and its flip side the pain-body disappear, many of your best personality traits and skills will remain because they were always a reflection of your true being and not from the ego that falsely claimed these qualities as its own.

Next time someone says to you, "Tell me about yourself," if you truly wish to tell them about yourself, see if you can identify the permanent, unchanging sense of being alive and aware beneath your shifting story of "me." Who you *are* is this aliveness, this awareness. When you come from this, you'll no longer find yourself dwelling on your grandiose ideas of yourself—and even less on all the things you've suffered.

---

[7] Tolle, Eckhart. *A New Earth,* Dutton, 2005, pp. 154-160.

3

THERE IS A DEEPER REALITY

There is more to this world than we typically perceive. If you are reading this book, you, like me, have probably been a lifelong seeker.

In my teens, I was fascinated by books about ghosts, to the point that a friend and I tried to record their voices in a graveyard at night! Later, books on fortune-telling led me to offer tarot card readings for fun. Then in the 1990s I became interested in energy healing, crystals, the power of visualization, and the wisdom traditions of indigenous peoples.

Although none of these explorations brought me the fulfillment I was seeking, diving into such interests eventually led to an awareness of a living energy field. I also discovered I possessed an ability to obtain inner guidance from what appeared to be a wiser part of me.

When I began toying with energy movement in my body, combining it with a homemade form of meditation, it resulted in some blissful and healing experiences that had me temporarily transcending my sense of myself as an individual.

Motivated by these unusual but pleasant states, I wanted to touch more of this apparent "other realm," so in 2000 I went on a fasting retreat in the Bavarian Alps. On the sixteenth day of what would be a thirty-three day fast, I experienced a long moment of sacred clarity. Everything I looked at in my hotel room seemed to "speak" back to me, revealing its true identity behind its physical disguise. It was as if the wall said it was God, the door handle said it was God, the bed said it was God, and my body said it was God. In other words, I was detecting a vibrant depth to everything.

Because I could actually *feel* this deeper dimension of reality, this profound moment of clarity I had experienced started me inquiring into who *I* really was, as well as wanting to understand what was behind these unusual and powerful experiences.

I want to emphasize that this experience of the depth dimension in everything wasn't like the euphoric highs I had encountered before I went to Bavaria. Instead, it was quietly powerful, deeply comforting, and revealed that the mysteries of life aren't so much "out there" in some magical realm, but right here in the most mundane events and objects. For this reason, after I returned home from Bavaria, my interest in pursuing peak experiences waned and I was more drawn to the simplicity of meditation.

Within a month of my return home, toward the end of 2000, I came across *The Power of Now* and immediately recognized that it was guiding me in the direction I needed to go. Eckhart Tolle's book pointed out that by becoming present, I could escape the incessant thinking and reacting of my mind. This would allow me to directly experience my deeper peaceful nature. I could wake up from the idea of "me," with its need to maintain a self-image, and simply *be*. When I took this step, it turned out that at the deepest level, I am—we all are—part of the awareness that's the source of all creation, the very thing I had experienced in Bavaria.

This realization had a profound effect on me. The grip my past had on me fell away. As it did so, my concerns about the future also began losing their hold on me. I still felt like *me,* but without needing my memories or dreams of tomorrow in order to have an identity. I was becoming more and more comfortable with the here and now, and found it was easy to remain present. In fact, it required quite a lot of effort to be lost in thought for any length of time.

Unlike Eckhart, my awakening didn't involve a traumatic event such as a "dark night of the soul" or some other kind of crisis. Though there was a point early on when I realized I'd had enough of talking, thinking, and reading about enlightenment and decided to "walk my talk" so to speak, the shift from identifying with my thoughts and emotions to living in the present happened gradually between 2001 and 2003.

So what you are describing is the same as believing in God, right?

Not exactly.

The problem with belief in God is that it tends to get in the way of the direct experience of God I've been speaking of. This is because the ego recreates God in its own image.

If you think about the gods and goddesses of various religions, they tend to be deities who need to be feared and worshipped. Often disapproving of the world and dissatisfied with humanity, they display the same emotional volatility as the ego of the individuals who invented such gods.

Not everyone believes in a God, of course. Nonbelievers simply believe in something else. The egoic mind doesn't care what we believe, as long as all of our attention is consumed by thought. Worshiping our thoughts keeps the false self alive just as well as worshiping some kind of God.

It may surprise you to hear that there's no more reason to believe in God than there's a need for you to believe in your hand. In fact, were I to ask you whether you believe in your hand, I'm sure you'd think it a strange question. That's because you don't need to believe in something that's always been part of your body. There's simply no point in "believing" in what you *know* to be a reality.

When someone asks "Do you believe in God?" of a person who experiences the divine, the question sounds as strange as asking if they believe in their hand. Such a person doesn't need to believe in God, since they know themselves to be an expression of God's own being. There's no need to keep thinking about what you experience continually—the fact that God *is*, and that at the deepest level God and humans are one.

Unlike the deities people generally worship, God has no shape or form, possesses no name, and has no gender and no body. Rather, this formless, dimensionless reality is the basis of our existence. You can test this for yourself by simply becoming fully attuned to the present moment. In the absence of mental noise and emotional turmoil, you'll begin to perceive your true nature, which turns out to be the formless awareness that's the source of everything.

To get an idea of what I mean when I speak of everything arising from the formless source, imagine traveling through a portion of outer space that's thick with stars and coming upon something which looks like a long black river from which no light can escape. From this spatial rift, a vapor-like mist constantly bubbles up and recedes back into its black source. The mist represents the potential birth of forms from this formless river. Any part of this mist that remains out long enough in the cold of deep space freezes into a form and moves out into the universe. The potential for existence has become actual, for a while at least. Formless permanence has created impermanent forms that in some cases may exist for a nanosecond and in others for billions of years.

You may not have thought of yourself as "one" with the formless source that gives rise to all forms in the way this image speaks of, and yet the direct experience of your boundless nature has always been available to you. By becoming aware of the present moment, the timelessness of each moment allows us to experience the formlessness of being itself.

If we had no beliefs, wouldn't there be suffering? Surely it's our beliefs that keep us from running amok.

Many see their beliefs as one of the most important aspects of their lives. However, the fact that billions of people hold firm beliefs hasn't kept our world free of suffering. On the contrary, one only has to look at the prevalence of personal and global suffering to recognize that chaos is a reality for most of humanity, despite their beliefs.

It's no coincidence that a world based on beliefs is rife with chaos and suffering. The problem is that humans identify with a set of thoughts, turning them into beliefs. Our beliefs then become the building blocks of the ego, which sees us as a world unto ourselves, separate from all others, and therefore free to indulge in cruelty toward our fellow humans, the creatures we share the world with, and the planet itself. It's this same false self that generates the unease, distress, and anguish so many of us experience.

Strongly held beliefs are often thought of as the basis of values. But these are themselves just notions about the "proper" way to conduct our lives. The personal and global suffering we witness everywhere is, however, evidence that a morality based on what certain people think—and tell us we should think—is a poor substitute for the natural morality that emerges spontaneously when we're grounded in the peaceful awareness that's our true self.

Awareness of what it means to live a harmonious life, along with a sense of when our life is out of balance, comes from beyond our thoughts. The natural morality inherent in existence itself emerges whenever the false self and its concepts of morality either fail or are no longer dominant. It's for this reason that the characteristics of awareness—such qualities as peace, wisdom, compassion, and joy—will form the basis of morality in the next stage in the evolution of human consciousness.

Wouldn't basking in a collective oneness prevent me from seeing anything as evil? I can't pretend everything is perfect when the world is full of terrible things.

Going through life mistaking the "voice in the head" for who we are contributes to a world of terrible things.

Once we recognize we are all expressions of a single formless reality, accusing another person of being bad is as useful as judging your hand to be bad. In fact, it's because the mental concepts of good and evil, right and wrong, reinforce the illusion that we are all separate entities, rather than expressions of a single reality, that they have always failed to produce the harmony we seek. Since one person's "good" or "right" is another person's "bad" or "wrong," the constant struggle to determine which is which has resulted in confusion, anguish, and endless violence on both a personal and global scale.

From the higher perspective of the formless awareness that's the source of everything—the oneness of which we are all a part—certain actions promote suffering while others promote peace. People who create suffering for themselves or others are unaware of what they are doing because they are unaware that they are ultimately one with the person they are afflicting. How aware we are of our true nature as part of the oneness from which everything has sprung determines whether we behave in ways that perpetuate the illusion of our separateness, or whether we embrace each other as manifestations of the intelligence that's the core of all reality. One path leads to suffering, the other to peace.

You could say that "good" is whatever promotes the peace that accompanies awareness of our true selves, whereas "evil" is whatever creates the suffering that results from resisting reality. However, because reality isn't quite so black and white, it's best to limit the use of words like good, bad, evil, right, and wrong to avoid unnecessary confusion and debate.

Couldn't everything you are speaking about just be part of the mind?

The reality I'm referring to exists beyond the limited version of it in our minds. This reality provides the space required for the mind to exist.

Consciousness doesn't need the mind in order to exist, whereas the mind can't exist without consciousness. Everything I'm saying is part of the mind because words are expressed thoughts. However, the reality that the words point to has nothing to do with the sounds coming from our mouths or the images in our heads.

Were the mind all there is, we wouldn't know it. This is because we require something that *isn't* mind in order to recognize that which *is* mind. For example, if you point to an object and declare, "That's a lamp," you are also recognizing—without saying as much—that things that aren't lamps also exist, including yourself.

The fact we can notice change is evidence of the presence of something permanent.[8] Without something permanent in the background to provide perspective and contrast, we wouldn't be able to perceive forms such as galaxies, people, places, nature, objects, events, thoughts, and emotions because these are all impermanent. However, this "something" in the background is actually "no-thing." Instead, it's awareness, and it notices everything.

One reason it may seem there's nothing beyond the mind is that the contents of the mind appear to be seamless, so that one thought runs into another. Thoughts and emotions combine to produce the story of "me" and the beliefs associated with this story. As our personal narrative becomes an impenetrable wall of content, we lose awareness of the silent space from which all thoughts and emotions emerge. To the degree we are incapable of noticing the spaces between our thoughts, we have lost touch with our true being. The story of "me" has supplanted the direct experience of our true nature. A subconscious fear that we would cease to exist were we to stop thinking keeps our attention fixed on the content of our minds.

Are you saying that attention and awareness are other ways of describing who I am?

Yes. These words describe that which has no form. The only thing that absolutely has no form is the awareness from which we have emerged and of which we are each a manifestation.

The concept of "attention" has been reduced to describing mental focus, when in fact to be truly alert requires a completely quiet mind. Attention is awareness, uniquely expressed in each of us. You might say that attention is awareness aware of itself.

Noticing the "voice in the head" is the beginning of the end for

---

[8] Tolle, Eckhart. *Stillness Speaks,* Namaste Publishing, 2003, pp. 110.

our ego, our false persona, with its need for beliefs and values based on thought, since its power is largely derived from going unnoticed. The story of "me" begins to dissolve piece by piece, and yet we are still here, alive and intact.

Over time, we realize awareness is more than just a peaceful refuge from our thought-induced anguish. We notice a very familiar feeling in this quiet place. It becomes clear that this peaceful space is our true identity.

WHAT EMOTIONS ARE REALLY ABOUT

Potentially our natural state is one of predominantly "no thought," in which an intelligent awareness runs life effortlessly and makes use of thinking only for brief periods before returning to the pure awareness of the present moment. This state already exists, awaiting our spiritual evolution to recognize it.

Emotions are in large measure a reaction to thought. Even when an emotion is triggered directly, before thought can kick in, it doesn't become a problem until we begin to tell ourselves a story about the situation. It only becomes problematic when the egoic mind begins to interpret, or rather misinterpret, what's occurring.

Emotions frequently trigger a physical effect. This happens because, as intelligent as the body is, it doesn't know that what's happening in our mind isn't actually happening outside of us. This is why thinking about a frightening situation can set the heart racing and cause us to sweat every bit as much as having a gun thrust in our face. However, when the body produces a physical reaction to a virtual event in the head, it isn't aligned with reality.

When thought is habitual or compulsive, what starts out as harmless emotional reactions to our thoughts can turn into a chronic state of unease. Incessant thinking pushes us out of alignment with our naturally peaceful state, and this is registered in the body as pressure and discomfort. Although the egoic mind tries to rid itself of the discomfort, it doesn't have much success because its very attempts to do so obscure the awareness that's our true state.

As long as we don't know who we are at our core, we remain out of alignment with ourselves. It's for this reason that self-help is never terribly successful. Positive images and affirmations provide only temporary relief because they don't touch the cause of our distress. In fact, repeated affirmations can worsen the problem, since they reinforce identification with thought, which in turn increases our alienation from ourselves. The more we attempt to think positively, the more frustrated we become when the relief we seek eludes us.

So you are against "positive thinking"?

We can use positive thinking briefly when we are still new to cultivating awareness of the present moment, but know that its benefits are limited and will provide diminishing returns.

Constant thinking produces a great deal of emotion. Even when our thoughts are positive, they are still producing emotion that often isn't aligned with what's actually happening. When thought and the emotion it can result in continues unchecked, what starts out as a mild unease may turn into distress, both mental and physical.

To alleviate our increased discomfort, the mind searches for solutions in the only place it knows—the world around us. This too proves futile, since everything around us is a form of some sort. We may seek out another person in the hope they'll make us feel happy. Or we may turn to alcohol, tobacco, tranquilizers, or some other compulsive activity or form of distraction. None of these work for long because only alignment with the formless awareness that's our true being can return us to a deep sense of wellbeing.

This becomes clearer when we observe an emotion disappear by simply attending to it—that is, feeling the physical reality of it. We neither say nor do anything to change the situation we believe has upset us, but instead go within to enter the present moment, in which a peaceful clarity reveals that our emotional wounds were largely self-inflicted. The discomfort we feel always has less to do with what's happening around us and more to do with the fact that our thoughts are resisting what's happening.

From our egoic perspective, it seems that resistance and rejection ought to move us away from pain and suffering. This is because we don't realize that resistance to something is still attachment to it. Our rejection of anything, including the body, pulls us more deeply into the abstract realm and guarantees our continued suffering.

An emotion can't sustain itself unless it's confined, constricted, and unobserved. However, observing an emotion directly, allowing it to be as it is, can be difficult because of the potent stories that are attached to our emotions—stories of which we are often unaware. Consequently, when we pay attention to the sensations an emotion produces and not the story attached to it, we create space that begins to dissipate it.

Whenever you begin to feel overwhelmed, move your attention to a peripheral body part such as your feet, the backs of your knees, or your elbows. Now, feel that peripheral part as deeply as possible. Notice there's little to no suffering beyond the borders of the emotion. However, you can still feel a sense of aliveness beyond these borders, which means you are not the emotion—not this "energy under pressure" that's largely confined to parts of the head and torso.

You are the tranquil space in which emotions, sensations, and thoughts happen. Move your attention back and forth from the center of the emotion to the peripheries of your body until the emotion dissipates and you feel safe and comfortable enough to rest your attention anywhere in your body.

Why does a wave of negativity sometimes wash over me for no reason at all?

Although such negativity appears not to have a cause, it in fact does have a cause. It's just that we are unable to observe the source of a particular emotion because our personal narrative is so seamless. Because one thought runs into another, the fact that our incessant thinking is producing constant emotional reactions goes largely unobserved—so much so that it's considered normal, and we imagine all these thoughts and the emotions they trigger are *who we are*. We then label them "me."

It isn't only the "thinker" that wishes to endure, but also the "reactor"—the *emotional* "me," since it's not only our thinking but the resulting emotions that constitute the ego and its flip side the painbody. Returning to the matter of abuse for a moment, this is why, at the sentencing of a famous entertainer, some of the individuals he preyed on said their lives were irreparably damaged. As one testified, even being touched inappropriately "took away from me that feeling that you can ever be normal again." Something that may have lasted only moments in this way becomes an identity.

The *emotional* "me" is largely made up of negativity that not even times of pleasure and satisfaction can overcome. Though masked temporarily, the general sense of unease that lies beneath the surface never goes away.

You say we can know our true nature by feeling it. Are you talking about emotions or physical sensations?

Although feelings can refer to both, I'm emphasizing physical sensations and a deep sense of wellbeing that transcends emotions. For example, the presence of peace may be registered in the body as a pleasant physical sensation. This pleasurable sensation results from a reduction of the pressure that's built up in the body from resisting what *is*.

However, the direct experience of our aware self includes more than a physical sensation. As our awareness moves through form toward formlessness, bodily sensations that are physical at the surface of reality feel less dense and more like an energy field. A deep "knowing" that we are more than this limited bodily form accompanies these physical sensations. The more we recognize our limitless being, the more we access feelings of peace, fulfillment, and joy.

Many think of joy as an emotion. Like peace, joy is inherent in who we are. It's a characteristic of our state of being, as is love, wisdom, and creativity. It doesn't originate from things that happen, but is uncaused. However, because it flows through us in a similar way to emotion, we tend to confuse the two. In fact, we generally assume joy is just a stronger version of the temporary emotion called happiness.

Peace may elicit an emotional reaction such as happiness, excitement, or relief, and yet—like joy—peace itself isn't an emotion. It's a characteristic of our very being. When we allow it to, the peace that's already everywhere makes its appearance. Although peace permeates this dimension, it's unaffected by it because it's the *source* of this dimension.

Think of how a fish doesn't know it's in water, since water is its total environment—unless, of course, it's a flying fish that can momentarily escape the water!

You may feel peace in your body just like an emotion, but one is your permanent nature and the other a temporary wave of energy passing through the body.

Our basic states could be thought of as the many faces of the divine. Or think of them as the many facets of a diamond. The diamond looks different from each angle because of the way light is refracted through each of its many facets. In a similar way, words like joy, peace, love, wisdom, and creativity describe the one source of everything from slightly different perspectives. The point is, because these states are always present, we can tune into them whenever we stop thinking.

The presence of any one of these states means that the ego has become inactivated for the time being. When it reappears, it invariably tries to make sense of the state we've just experienced. It may categorize it as a "transcendent" experience, not realizing that what feels transcendent is actually our normal state.

If it's one of many states of being, then why emphasize peace?

When we are coming from ego, instead of from our true being, we are completely absorbed in the mind's movements—that is, in our thoughts and emotional reactions—to the point that we begin to believe the content of our mind is who we are.

Our intention is to move away from thought and emotional reactivity. But we don't want to do this in a hostile, "fighting" frame of mind. On the contrary, it's important not to forget that this incessant mental activity is our starting point on the path to the peace that's to be found only in the present moment.

The deeper we go into the experience of peace, the easier it is to come to rest in the moment. Attending to the stillness of peace is very helpful in quieting the movements of our mind—our thoughts and emotional reactions. Whenever we enter into this stillness, we become aware of our true nature as *being*.

Love and joy, which like peace are characteristics of our very being, are typically perceived as moving experiences. On the surface, love and joy can feel like emotions. For this reason, it's easy to confuse them with the mind's movements.

To make sure we aren't fooled by the mind's movements—by our thoughts masquerading as awareness or our emotions mimicking the deeper states of love, joy and peace—we can focus on the stillness of peace directly. For some of us this might prove a little daunting at first, however.

There's an alternative approach we can all use quite easily. A fundamental aspect of peace is its subtlety. You might say it's the nature of peace to be the least of things. For this reason, when we focus on the most subtle of forms, it's easier to observe the thoughts and emotional reactions we experience, and come to recognize that we are the witnessing presence to these movements and not the mental activity itself.

What does it mean to focus on the most subtle of forms? We're speaking of such things as listening to your own breath, seeking out the quietest sounds in your immediate environment, softening your gaze to notice the empty space around you and perhaps the speck of dust floating in the air, noticing the empty space around the letters on this page, or stepping outside and listening to the sound of birds or the breeze.

In other words, whenever we go deep into any experience, including our moving experiences, we cannot help but find the peaceful stillness within them. We recognize the permanent and "unmoved being" that we are.

When something truly amazing or shocking happens, my emotional response is the result of an actual event, not a thought.

The initial excitement or shock isn't a problem. It's what we do with it next as we begin thinking about it. As long as we're heavily identified with our thoughts and emotions, we tend to react with a mental interpretation, such as approval or disapproval, acceptance or rejection.

To the egoic mind, there's little perceivable difference between abstract thought and genuine reality. However, genuine reality is uninterpreted reality. In this state, we experience what *is* from our natural condition of *no thought*. Without the filter of interpretations, reactions, or a false sense of "me," we perceive things the way they are. All of the things that make up our lives, including our body, then appear to be surface representations of a much deeper mystery.

The feelings we experience point to an even deeper reality that's imperceptible to the senses. In other words, the peace and joy we experience are only the tip of the iceberg, since the human body limits the extent to which we can experience the whole of the underlying reality of which we are expressions.

If you think about a flower, it emits a fragrance comprised of the same molecules as the flower itself. The fragrance is actually a physical extension of the flower beyond its petals. We know there's a flower in our midst even in a completely dark room where we can't see it. The point is that there's much more to the flower than just its fragrance. The fragrance is merely one aspect, one dimension of a flower's existence. In the same way, the peace-filled knowing we experience is a small taste of the mysterious awareness from which everything has arisen. The body that enables us to experience our formless nature also limits this same experience.

Our ideas about peace have little to do with the reality of peace. Even when we come to know peace through direct experience, we become aware of how great a mystery it will always be.

Consider the infinite intelligence that's ultimately the whole of reality. There's no way to get outside of it in order to perceive it, since it includes everything. It *has* no "outside." As long as we are finite, our experience of the ultimate oneness of reality will always be limited.

Although we may no longer identify with the body as if it was all we are, we still sense and perceive things through it. The more deeply we immerse ourselves in the experience of pure awareness, the less we think of ourselves as our body and the more we know and understand our true nature. Yet, just as the flower doesn't in any way disown its fragrance, neither does the person who is in touch with their deeper self disown their body. They simply recognize that it's only a temporary expression of who they really are.

As long as I identify with the thinker in my head, I feel I need concepts and metaphors to point me in the right direction.

Then let me give you another. Follow me in the following conversation:

"Have you looked out the window today?" someone asks.

"Yes. It's overcast at this moment," another replies.

"But would you say there's still plenty of daylight?"

"Of course. It's early afternoon."

"Since we're in agreement that there's plenty of daylight, can you point out some of this daylight to me?"

The person gestures toward the sky and responds, "The daylight is everywhere, all around us."

"You were sort of vaguely pointing into space. But can you point out a specific piece of this daylight?"

"Hmm. No, I guess I can't. It isn't something we can divide into pieces or hold in our hands."

Like daylight, peace is one indivisible whole, a single phenomenon that's everywhere at once. Just as there isn't *my* daylight or *your* daylight, Manhattan daylight or Miami Beach daylight, neither is there *my* peace or *your* peace. The peace in Times Square is the same as the peace in Tiananmen Square, although it won't be recognized until someone experiences it.

In the same way that we have the ability to step out of a dark room and experience daylight, we can step out of the darkness of our unconsciousness—our lack of awareness—and experience our true nature, which is peace.

If you stop to consider, you'll realize we can't actually see daylight at all. We can only see what it comes in contact with. We can look around and see the objects, people, and places that daylight reflects off, and these tell us of its presence even though in itself it's invisible. Well, peace is much like daylight in the sense that it's often only recognized by what it illumines.

A person illumined by peace realizes they aren't *merely* their mind and body. They can now see clearly that they are in fact one with peace itself. This is why, observing an enlightened person, a deep serenity seems to emanate from them. They also display a gentle acceptance of people and each of the many situations they find themselves in. There's no resistance.

Daylight is the evidence on a cloudy day of something greater in our midst, which is, of course, the sun. Daylight, which is comprised of the sun's rays, is the physical extension of the sun itself. Just as daylight isn't manufactured by anyone on this planet, the deep peace we feel inside us isn't something we manufacture either. Rather, it's evidence of the presence of an ultimate reality that is itself peaceful awareness. And even as there's no ultimate distinction between the sun and its rays, there's ultimately no distinction between the peace we experience and the source of peace.

These examples are intended to take us beyond a mind that thinks it can grasp everything. Be aware of the mind's tendency to overvalue and cling to words that point to our true nature without trying to apply them and embody them. The high regard the mind has for itself is revealed in our use of the expression "to be out of your mind" in reference to insanity. In reality, insanity is the state of being obsessively *in* your mind, completely identified with your own thoughts.

Believing we are the "voice in the head" results in great personal suffering, not to mention the cruel and irrational behavior that results in global suffering. Only when we step out of our minds and become aware of reality can we finally see the madness of our ways and experience peace.

In conclusion, we could say that the "peace of mind" we seek is actually the peace of *no mind*.

5

INTRODUCING YOUR "OFF" SWITCH

Thankfully, life provides us with a kind of "off" switch for the software that forever runs in our minds. This off switch is the body.

As physical bodies, we are surrounded by countless shapes and forms, ranging from mountains, lakes, oceans, forests, fields, and deserts to our own creations in the form of cities, transport, and communications. With such a wealth of things to fascinate us, it's easy to become so engrossed in the world beyond our body that we forget the body is our primary geography.

When we lose touch with our own person-shaped landscape, we go through life only partially and peripherally feeling our body. In this state, the physical sensations we experience appear connected to particular body parts and organs. We don't realize that, at a greater depth, these surface sensations are manifestations of a single living energy field. A growing number of people have an awareness now that it's possible to feel this subtle aliveness all the time.

It's this split, this divergence of body and mind, that we experience as a lack of peace. Part of us is here, while part of us isn't. Divided against ourselves in this way, we're bound to feel anxious.

The good news is that even though, in our head, we may be elsewhere, the body is always here in the present moment. We may be lost in thought or caught up in an emotional reaction, but if we turn our attention away from our thoughts and emotions by feeling the physical sensations in our body, we automatically find ourselves becoming present—and with presence comes peace.

Said differently, to be present is to be anchored in the *real*. Grounded in reality, we are less prone to the judgments and reactions that produce distress and thereby block our awareness of the peace that's the essence of our makeup.

It's as if becoming present bores holes in the mind content that's been walling us in, opening up space between our thoughts and emotions. Because our personal narrative is no longer a seamless, impenetrable stream of thought, we gain the ability to distinguish between what's real and what's imaginary, and so at last stop torturing ourselves with our thoughts and the emotions they generate.

Aren't thoughts part of reality?

Thoughts are a *reference* to the actual, the real. We might think of them as a simulation. As such, they are an abstract copy of the original, which is something that can be experienced only in the reality of the present moment.

To illustrate by returning to an example cited earlier, no words, images, or thoughts about a grapefruit can compare to the taste, smell, and texture of an actual grapefruit, which can only be enjoyed as we are eating it. Direct experience only ever happens *now*.

The present moment, which we can access through deep body awareness, is the off switch to the thinker and its endless narrative of "me and my story." When the mind is quiet, a deeper intelligence and stillness emerges, and we realize this peaceful state has always been here. It's often referred to as "the peace of God," and we now recognize it as the peace of being one with the intelligence that birthed the cosmos.

Can't I just focus on the present moment in order to become peaceful?

Who would be doing the focusing? It would be the ego, the imposter that prefers to turn techniques into a mental exercise. It has no interest in, and is actually a little threatened by, becoming aware of the body.

Some people choose to focus on a mantra, a candle, a flower, or some other object to distract themselves from thought. Here again, you would be using your mental software to try to focus on the present—the very action that prevents you from being aware.

Whenever we begin our assessment of reality from the default position of thought, we are incapable of determining what's abstract versus what's actual. Thought comes between us and reality, tricking us into believing we are perceiving the present moment clearly, when in fact we aren't. Since using the mind as a filter distorts our perception of reality, thinking about the present actually moves us further away from the awareness we seek and the peace that accompanies it.

In contrast, the body is always part of our current surroundings, always part of what *is*. Since it's always in the present moment, it's our base reference for reality—the key to distinguishing between what's real and what's imaginary such as the stories we tell ourselves in our head. To disregard our body is to continue resisting reality, so that awareness of our inherently peaceful state becomes impossible.

Although awareness of the body is essential for discovering our true nature, paradoxically we aren't the physical body we perceive ourselves to be. By attending to the body, we begin to *feel* the realization that we aren't simply the body.

The fact that what we truly are can be felt, not thought, is why feeling our body is so important. In the quest for either personal peace or world peace, the body can't be bypassed. We must go *through* the body to go beyond the body and directly experience the peace that's our nature.

When we go through the body to go beyond it to our peaceful essence, we realize we are each an expression of the infinite space in which the body, the mind, and all other shapes and forms exist. We are attention itself, the silent observer behind and within everything. We are the one who observes the interaction between objects, thoughts, and emotions from the "inside" as well as the "outside," so to speak. Looking into the empty space around you will give you a better idea of what you are than looking in the mirror.

Like the air we breathe, peace is both within us and around us. In other words, peace isn't personal, any more than breathing air into our lungs makes it "my" air. As we become aware that peace has no form and isn't tied to any particular place, time, or experience, we also realize our existence isn't limited to the physical body. We will then see for ourselves that peace can be found in all people, objects, and events.

Beneath the surface turmoil of the world is peace. Knowing we are all part of this universal peace guides our behavior and inspires us to create the physical manifestations and social structures of global peace and harmony.

If it's so important to feel the body, how can I be sure I'm really feeling it?

The *felt* experience of the body will help you realize you are much more than your limited mental version of "me and my body." To give you some sense of what this feels like, right now, are you feeling your feet? If you pay attention to your feet, you'll probably find you begin feeling them, at least a little. Now, can you feel them from the "inside," so to speak? Can you feel a subtle energetic tingling—an aliveness—within every part of them? People often tell me they can feel certain parts of their feet, particularly where the skin is in contact with their socks or shoes.

Fully inhabiting the body begins when we can feel physical sensations without generating mental interpretations or emotional reactions to those sensations. We find ourselves simply looking, listening, and being. In this quiet space, if we keep our attention on our physical sensations, we feel the body as a vibrant energy field of aliveness that paradoxically also has the quality of the deep stillness that's characteristic of the present moment. It's possible to feel this subtle aliveness throughout the body almost all of the time, even during a conversation or when engaged in an activity.

Cultivating presence through deep body awareness isn't something most people find easy because the egoic mind resists anything that could lead to its dissolution. However, when we relax the body, it becomes easier to feel the aliveness within it. With our attention anchored in this aliveness, the mind becomes quiet and we return to the present moment. In this state, we can go about our normal day-to-day lives without becoming reactive to either the people around us or events that happen. Neither do we replay the loop of dysfunctional thinking about our unhappy past or uncertain future.

Once you are truly feeling your body, there will be little to no uncomfortable pressure in your body because there will be virtually no resistance to what *is*. There will be no psychological pressure from wanting the next moment or from reflecting on what could or should have been. The presence of a vibrant peace and mental clarity will accompany you regardless of the situation you find yourself in.

What if my body feels uncomfortable?

Life not only uses words, art, and nature to awaken us from the dream of "me," it also uses physical discomfort to inform us we are resisting the reality of the present moment.

When we experience the body through the filter of the mind, life sends a message of physical discomfort telling us we're out of alignment with reality. In other words, it's indicating to us that our awareness of what *is*, which includes the body, has become only partial and peripheral. The discomfort continues to increase in intensity the longer we remain lost in the abstract realm of thought and emotion.

Often the mental "me" misinterprets this signal and concludes we need to tune the body out, when in reality the suffering body is actually asking us to give it more high quality attention, not less. The body doesn't really want the excess entertainment, food, sex, drugs, pharmaceuticals, or the new clothes, houses, cars, and so on that we expose it to in order to temporarily ease our suffering. It wants attention from our essential being, because all suffering ends when we return to peace.

Indeed, when we are deeply present, we are so at peace that no psychological suffering is possible.

When we are in the grip of the mental "me," it can seem like we are feeling our body *too* much, to the point it can be unbearable to be in the body. However, what's "too much" is our mental resistance to reality, which reverberates in the body as emotional suffering.

You say we don't have to suffer. But what about physical pain?

Accidents and injuries are a part of life. Pain is inevitable. However, as we experience pain, we can also feel the reassuring comfort of a deep peace beneath the pain. Completely accepting what *is*, including the pain, allows for the emergence of peace. In a sense, the space that's created reduces the intensity of the energy under pressure, which is what pain is. Even emotional pain from a recent sense of loss can be felt, accepted, and allowed to pass through us rather quickly.

The pain that comes from long-term mental and emotional reactions to what happened in the past or may happen in the future is different. This is suffering, and it can be avoided. When we are present, pain doesn't turn into a "victim story" that then adds to our identity as a victim—an identity made up of unresolved pain from our past that's become chronic psychological and emotional suffering. If our mind-made suffering continues to go unobserved, the suffering that results can manifest as bodily pain or illness.

Regardless of pain's origins—a recent physical injury or old emotional wound—to inhabit the present moment increases our awareness of peace, which in turn reduces the intensity of the pain we feel.

When you speak of the mind, does that include the brain?

Sometimes, in casual conversation, people use these words interchangeably, although in reality they are different.

The brain is the physical counterpart of the energy field of the mind, the latter being of a higher frequency than the world of solid objects. The brain is the primary way in which we as physical beings participate in the universal field of consciousness, whereas the mind is localized consciousness that has been conditioned by its proximity to the brain it makes use of. We might think of the mind as a virtual drawing board on which our understanding of reality is worked out. Functioning like a simulator, it recreates reality as a hologram that facilitates reflection and analysis.

The virtual is designed to help us navigate reality—although, since it tends to focus on analyzing the past and worrying about the future, it's extremely limited in its ability to understand reality. Past and future are thoughts and images that refer to reality but have no existence outside of our head. We can no more find a piece of future in the grass than we can drink a cold cup of past. Past and future only appear to have concrete existence because the mind agrees with other people's minds to make use of our "time" software. We overlay this time-measuring program onto reality without realizing we are doing so.

To get an idea of the role of the mind, think of the icons that appear all over the screen of a digital camera, indicating the time, date, amount of light, shutter speed, and so on. They are there to help us measure the reality we are looking at through the viewfinder. Are these icons printed directly onto the person, mountain, or house you are photographing? No, they aren't part of reality but are simply concepts.

In a similar manner, we behave as if clock numbers are a natural feature of the blue sky and as if mountains come into being with height measurements physically etched into their rock. For convenience, we label earth's rotations, though we can never touch Thursday or hold this year in our hands because they are only ideas. There is only the continuous flow of life, happening now. If we left life alone, simply allowing it to be without our interpreting filter, we would experience it as the wondrous reality it is.

Since it's largely cut off from our awareness of the body, our sense of self has retreated to the area above the neck associated with the brain. However, discoveries in new medical fields such as neurocardiology and neurogastroenterology reveal that the brain isn't limited to the space in our head. The nervous system embedded in the lining of the gastrointestinal tract is in fact now recognized as *a brain in its own right*.[9] We literally feel and "know" with our gut.

It's also estimated that more than half of all heart cells are neurons like those found in our brain. These cluster in "small neural groupings connected through the same type of axon-dendrites forming the neural fields of our brain."[10] The heart not only communicates with the rest of the body through these neural connections, but it also has a direct neural connection to the limbic system of the brain.[11] So while the brain informs and directs the heart, the heart similarly informs and directs the brain. For this reason, bringing awareness into our heart area is essential if we are to make use of our entire brain. As the heart becomes open and relaxed, the rest of the body also becomes more receptive.

Maybe the heart can inform the brain about the condition of organs and other physiological processes. What role can the heart play in understanding philosophy, architecture, music theory, or mathematics?

The way the brain system extends throughout the body mirrors the mind's energy field, which both permeates and encompasses the body. In a sense, then, you use your whole body to understand things, including the words you are reading now. So when you restrict awareness of your body, you restrict your brain, which in turn limits what the mind can comprehend.

Constriction of the heart area in particular dulls awareness and limits comprehension. The "heart area" includes not only the chest, which contains the heart and lungs, but also the energy field around the heart. While there's much more for science to discover about the

[9] Gershon, Michael. "The Enteric Nervous System: A Second Brain," Hospital Practice, Volume 34, No.7, abstract, http://www.hosppract.com/index. php?article=153.
[10] Pearce, Joseph Chilton. T*he Biology of Transcendence: A Blueprint of the Human Spirit,* Park Street Press, 2002, p. 64.
[11] Ibid.

subtle energy of the heart, researchers are now able to measure heart energy frequencies. The heart produces an electromagnetic field that saturates the body with its energy frequencies and extends outward up to fifteen feet.[12] An electrocardiogram is actually able to pick up this energy field from three feet away without any electrodes touching the body.

This energy field is holographic in nature, meaning that any point within the field "contains the information of the whole field."[13] In other words, scientists are now discovering what sages have intuited for thousands of years—that the heart is the doorway to the whole of reality. In fact, scientists speculate that everything that has shape and form, from atoms to planets and the universe itself, possess a holographic energy field whose totality exists within any part.

The energy field generated by the heart is the body's primary portal through which we retrieve the higher intelligence of pure awareness. Eastern philosophic traditions think of it as a vortex, known as a "chakra," through which the peace, love, and wisdom characteristic of universal awareness infuse the body.

Whereas limited body awareness means limited self-awareness, the more open and receptive the body is, the more the heart accelerates the comprehension process by helping us go beyond the physical realm to access the universal intelligence from which everything arises.

Information, knowledge, and aptitudes don't start out as abstract concepts, but begin as energy projected from the source of all knowing, pure awareness. Though we may not realize it, when we truly understand something, we briefly experience our inherent oneness with the energy frequency of the subject or skill we are focused on. This appears in the mind as insight, which can then be developed into understanding, knowledge, and skill. Having ready access to such insight counters our anxiety when we don't know what to do, adding greatly to our ability to be at peace in any and all situations.

In other words, as well as creating meaning and context from the

---

[12] Pearce, Joseph Chilton. *The Biology of Transcendence: A Blueprint of the Human Spirit*, Park Street Press, 2002, p. 57.
[13] Ibid., p. 58.

raw perceptual data provided by the brain, the heart's energy field can bypass the localized, conditioned consciousness of the mind and provide us with access to the wisdom inherent in the field of universal awareness. The more fully we align with this field, the greater our comprehension of any single aspect of it.

A heart that makes use of the entire range of available frequencies can also resonate with the field of any other form and align with its essence. Given all the misunderstandings that occur between human beings, imagine the peace this resonance brings to a person's relationships.

Does this mean that when I learned 2+2=4, I was using my heart and body to merge with the equation?

When you moved beyond rote memory and actually understood that 2+2=4, your body—the heart area in particular—relaxed and opened up briefly to give you access to the universal energy field in which all information exists.

Since no one was sufficiently self-aware to point out your body's role in comprehending this equation, all credit went to the brain in your head. However, had you known what to look for, you would likely have experienced a sigh along with an "Ah ha" or gentle "Ah," accompanied by an expansive feeling. It's quite common for people to make such sounds when they finally understand something.

It's no accident that these are also the sounds people make when expressing relief. Relief arrives as less pressure in the body, and thus less resistance to reality.

In terms of 2+2=4, we could say that your energy frequency harmonized with the frequency of this specific equation, as well as the universal principles of combining and totaling that are subfields embedded in this formula's energy field. You not only learned this specific equation, but you also deepened your understanding of how things can be measured and how they relate to each other.

After such an epiphany, the rapid return of the egoic filter and the layers of protection around the heart, which are a form of resistance, limits our ability to convert a holistic "knowing" into information that's meaningful to the mind. Therefore, the longer we can keep the body relaxed, and hence the heart receptive, the more comprehensive is our understanding. In other words, to fully know anything requires less mind and more embodiment.

Having said this, it's important to reiterate something touched on in an earlier chapter. While we may have a deeper appreciation for a person, object, experience, or concept, no amount of information could ever create a full understanding of something whose deepest nature is formless and therefore unknowable to the mind.

Invisible waves surround us carrying libraries of information to and from our radios, televisions, phones, and computers. In the same way, the highest intelligence and wisdom from the universal awareness is carried to us on waves of love and peace. Not only can we go into our body to cultivate present moment awareness and the peace that accompanies it, but we can also turn inward to access the most advanced information the universe has to offer. This includes practical information to help us in our daily life, solutions to global problems, and creative genius that will pave the way for the world of our dreams.

While directing our attention to any part of the body can quiet the mind, feeling the heart area is particularly effective when it comes to seeing through the veil of mind content. An open heart creates an open mind.

Can you help me become more aware of my body right now?

To fully inhabit the body and live in the present moment isn't actually a *doing*, but the *undoing* of the false persona. You don't need to create a state of peace, just to let go of those things that block awareness of your naturally peaceful self.

Think about it this way. You "practice" being the false "me" all day without realizing you're doing so. Cultivating presence through body awareness acts as a counterweight to all the many hours of the day you are engaged in your personal narrative.

One of the reasons mental agitation interferes with body awareness and the peace that comes with it is that we don't create sufficient gaps in our stream of thoughts, which of course contains our personal story of "me." Even those who attempt to inhabit their body tend to limit their practice of awareness to one or two brief periods, such as morning and evening. This allows the egoic mind to operate unhindered for the majority of the day.

The answer is to bring awareness into every part of our lives. There are ways to pull ourselves out of our thoughts and emotions, so that we notice the peaceful clarity of the present moment whether we are grocery shopping or watching television, at work or in traffic. By cultivating body awareness frequently throughout the day, we reduce the mental agitation that inhibits deeper body awareness.

In turn, this causes us to realize we can function efficiently without our mental software being constantly engaged. Over time, we develop a trusting relationship with the peaceful clarity that at first is a welcome refuge from our incessant thinking and reacting. Eventually, we recognize this vibrant stillness as our deepest essence.

Later in the book, we'll go into detail concerning the ways in which we can use the body to become aware. For now, pausing from time to time to unclench your muscles and feel your breathing will allow you to access the peace that comes with being present in each moment. As you read, after each chapter, check your jaw, shoulders, and solar plexus, unclenching them when necessary. Feel the movement of air in your nostrils and throat. Also, see if you can physically sense the clothing you are wearing.

The key is to pay more attention to the sensations in the body than to your thoughts and reactions about what you are doing. The alertness required to feel the reality of physical sensations will help you enter the peace-infused clarity of the present moment.

6

THE ROLE OF YOUR BODY IN AWAKENING TO PEACE

Having emphasized the importance of the body, it's equally important to understand that *you are not your body.*

Because the body is a miraculous wonder of beauty and genius that reflects the love and wisdom of the universal awareness of which we are all a part, it's understandable that, in addition to mistaking ourselves for the mind, we would also think of ourselves as the body.

That in our essential being we aren't the body can be seen by examining the temporary nature of the body. To illustrate, the body you have today isn't the same body you had as a child. Not only have you increased in size and your appearance changed, but almost every cell of your body has been replaced multiple times. Consequently, you don't have the same skin, same hair, same eyes, same fingernails, same blood, or even the same bones. Despite all these changes, the sense of "me" has remained all these years. It's as if life periodically gives you a full body transplant, so to speak. Although the body you now inhabit is very different from the one you had when you were a child, are you not still uniquely you?

Millions of people walk around on this planet without an appendix, and yet they are still a complete person. Others have had their spleen removed, their gallbladder taken out, or perhaps donated a kidney. Not only our kidneys, but also our liver and lungs can be replaced by those of someone else. None of this changes our experience of being ourselves.

If you had no arms, legs, or eyes, would you still respond if some- one called out your name? Of course you would. In fact, someone with considerably fewer body parts goes through life and experiences themselves as a person just like anyone else. And, as we know from the new technique of face transplants, even your face could be taken from another human, yet you would still respond to your name.

It's true that you can't exist without a heart. However, you could receive someone else's heart, or an artificial heart, and you would still exist. You need a heart to remain alive, but it doesn't have to be the heart with which you were born. In fact, there have been many documented cases of heart recipients taking on some of the behavior of donors. Yet all of these donor and recipient characteristics exist at the surface of reality. Any new traits that were "transplanted" along with the heart are no more who the person truly is than their original tendencies.

What about my brain? Isn't that unique to me?

Until recently the brain was believed to have a fixed number of neurons and an unchanging structure. The science of brain plasticity has radically altered this view. Researchers have learned brain cells are replaced even in old age.

In addition, cells that may have once been an integral part of our mental processes die off when our thoughts and actions create new pathways that leave those cells without a purpose.[14] Neurologist John Lorber discovered that patients with hydrocephalus were able to function normally even though significant portions of their brains had been compressed or crushed. These discoveries challenged the notion that a particular brain function always comes from a fixed brain location. Some of Lorber's patients were able to process images and see normally even though they had no visual cortex.[15]

---

[14] Doidge, Norman. *The Brain That Changes Itself,* Viking, 2007, pp. 250-255.
[15] Lewin, Roger. "Is Your Brain Really Necessary?" *Science,* December 12, 1980, Volume 210, pp1232-1234. (www.rifters.com/real/articles/Science_No-Brain.pdf). Also see David Paterson's article of the same name in World Medicine, 3 May, 1980, 21-24.

You might wonder whether you would still recognize your history if you had a different brain. Would you still like the same things, or would a different brain be a complete personality transplant? Well, does someone who has amnesia cease to exist? Life still animates their body. The person also continues to have a distinct perspective, a unique angle of view. All that's changed is their thoughts about themselves, their old identity replaced by a new one.

In the case of an amnesiac, neither the story of who they were before they experienced amnesia nor their new story is who they truly are. Identities can come and go. The thought that "I am this character" or "I am that character" may change, but the sense of "I Am" never disappears.

When you were four years old, you essentially had no history to speak of, although you still had a sense of being a person. And haven't you already had a "personality transplant" since you were four, or fourteen for that matter? For instance, do you still behave the same way and like the same things you did then? Even if you've greatly changed from some of the ways you were when you were young, the sense of being *you* is still there.

The storyless sense of "me" you had as a child was grounded in pure awareness, which became obscured as your "story of me" was superimposed over the awareness. When the story disappears, you continue to exist. Nothing can ever make who you truly are disappear—not even death.

From your current perspective, you appear to be a mind that possesses a solid body. However, not only are you not the body you perceive yourself to be, but neither are you the history your ego has created for your body.

The mistake is to build our story of "who I am" around our body and its heritage. For instance, when we tell the story of our life, we often begin with our biological parents or grandparents—and some even go to great lengths to trace their heritage back several generations. Still, no matter how far back we go, we are barely scratching the surface of our biological lineage, which actually stretches back a vast amount of time—not just to the beginning of the human species, but to the appearance of the first forms of life on earth, and beyond that all the way to the birth of the universe itself.

Understanding that we are not the "thinker" doesn't by itself dislodge the many conscious and unconscious assumptions we have regarding who we are. The awareness of our true, vibrant nature has been dulled by the incessant noise and calculations of the thinking mind.

I feel no connection to ancestors from centuries past. I start with my immediate family history when describing myself because they are the people I am most familiar with and the people I love. Even though I shouldn't be so attached to the body, the body enables us to distinguish one from another. For example, I can't experience what you are experiencing, and the body is clearly a factor in this.

None of us can experience what it's like to be in another person's body. Not only can we not experience what another person's body feels like, we can't even sense most of what's happening in our own body. For instance, can you feel your nails and hair growing at this moment? What about your cells dividing? How about the neurons firing in your brain? Even though we can't feel these processes that are going on all the time inside us, they are nevertheless a part of us.

What you were born to do, no one else can do for you. No one can feel your body for you. No one can distinguish between reality and abstract thought for you. No one can experience for you the peace that you are. This is something you must do for yourself. As you do so, you invite others to enter into this same experience for themselves. Then, instead of believing we are separate and seeing others as a potential threat to our survival, we will begin to see the beauty in each other.

Why is a particular person or a particular thing pleasing to us? On one level, many factors come into play—psychological, physiological, cultural conditioning, our personal history, and our genetic makeup. However, these factors don't take into account the deeper reason something feels good to us.

Whenever we aren't in alignment with our true nature, the resistance we feel to our circumstances generates discomfort in the body. Anyone or anything that alleviates this discomfort, at least for a while, tends to feel pleasing. Naturally, we credit this particular form for making us feel better. What we don't realize is that to feel good is our *natural* state, and the form we associate with a pleasant feeling is simply resonating with this deeper state, making us temporarily aware of it. The fact is, no other form is required to experience the peace, joy, and ease of being that's our nature.

When we feel unconditional love for someone, such as our family members, we are experiencing this resonance between our deepest being and their deepest being, which are one and the same.

The mind misperceives this deeper truth and instead weaves together a story based on the psychological, emotional, and biological bonds between bodies. While it's true we may be fond of and attached to a particular body, over time this body changes and may even lose much of what first appealed to us. However, our love for the person continues because what we really love about them are their essential qualities, which are unique expressions of the one reality in which we all participate.

To understand what we mean by "unique expressions of the one reality in which we all participate," imagine a beam of light that strikes the surface of water to create millions of sparkling points of light. The shimmering reflections are temporary phenomena, appearing and disappearing as the water moves. Each one seems to have an independent existence, yet all are products of the same singular light source. Now look around you. Many of the shapes or forms you see, including your body, appear independent of every other form. Yet just like the beam of light, they are all made of the same formless essence. Though the source of these forms is hidden, they are God disguised as creation.

Awakened to our true nature, we perceive our relationship with the body—and with all other bodies—as a seamless union of formlessness with form. This "recognition of oneness"[16] can leave us speechless. For this reason, the more we truly know something, the less we are able to

------

[16] Tolle, Eckhart. *A New Earth, Dutton,* 2005, p. 106.

describe it. It feels like love, since experiencing oneness is what love is. We recognize the other is one with us in essence. As the distinction between *I* and *other* begins to disappear, *two* realize they are essentially *one*. As their love continues to deepen, a vibrant peace emerges.

How can I experience not only my own true being, but that of others?

An excellent question, and an even better meditation.

Several billion people on this planet believe their essence is contained in a soul or spirit. In other words, most of us already sense at some level that we are more than the body, even though we often behave as if the body is all we are.

This contradiction ought to lead people inward to explore its mystery. But so far in humanity's sojourn on this planet, few have discovered the body as the portal that leads to the experience of God. For most, the belief that we are more than just a body has resulted in the rejection and denial of the body. Once again, it's our beliefs about the body and God that get in the way of the direct experience of the body and God.

What does it mean to go "inward" to explore the mystery of the body?

There has been a long-standing assumption among many spiritual seekers that self-inquiry is an intellectual pursuit. In truth, self-inquiry is a *felt* experience. A knowing—an intuitive *felt* understanding—arises in the body, through which we realize we aren't just the impermanent form that undergoes growth and decay.

In other words, "know thyself" isn't a matter of holding a concept of yourself, but is a direct experience. Any analysis beyond this is secondary. So when you inquire within, don't look to your thoughts for an answer, but go beyond thought to that which is formless.

When we stop playing the game of "me," we allow reality to come into focus. A quiet mind gradually reveals that we are not only here as a form, but that we can be found everywhere. We are more than the sum of our parts—more than our mind, our body, this planet, and every other created form. We are more than the physical universe itself because we are beyond form.

Because in our true identity we are part of the formless universal awareness from which everything has sprung, deep within each of us is a silent intelligence that already knows not only our own true being but also that of others. We intuitively know we are the peaceful awareness that brings these wonderful bodies and minds to life and uses them to explore its creation. We can connect with this silent intelligence whenever we choose to leave the conceptual world and return to the reality of the here and now.

Whether we want to or not, we are all moving on to the next stage of our development. The progression from spiritual adolescence to maturity can't be stopped, although it can be delayed. We can hold onto the false belief that we are our minds and bodies, or we can greatly reduce our suffering by accepting our collective oneness.

Today, as never before, it's vital we take the next step in our natural development sooner rather than later. This next step in our evolution isn't a larger cranium. Rather, we are currently undergoing an evolution of consciousness, moving beyond seeing ourselves as only body or mind and recognizing that we are the undying awareness from which these have come into existence.

You say we are all moving on to the next stage of our development. But what if I die before our species takes this leap? Where does that leave me?

The experience of death is misunderstood because we tend to perceive it through the filter of thoughts and emotions. When the body ceases to function, the life that you are continues but can no longer use the body as a vehicle to explore reality and express itself. Life has removed one of its temporary disguises, as it were.

We don't perceive the aliveness in someone who has died for the same reason we can't perceive life right now. Identification with the mind and the body blocks our awareness of their eternal nature. The good news, if we can say that, for the one whose body is dying is that it won't be long before they will know for themselves that life goes on. It's simply preferable and less painful that we discover this while the body is vibrant and functioning, since so much of the anxiety we experience as humans revolves around our fear of dying. When we are no longer afraid of the death of the body because we understand our eternal nature, great peace arises.

A word of caution may be necessary at this point. Because the body is only a temporary expression of who we are, some think of it as an illusion. In one sense, you could say it is. But just because the body isn't our ultimately real self doesn't mean we can jump off a tall building without getting killed.

Confusing absolute reality with the relative perception of forms is a frequent hazard on the path to self-discovery. Forms are real in the sense they are made up of the same formless consciousness that's derived from source itself. The illusion is that these forms are all we are. While it's true who we truly are can't ultimately be tarnished or damaged, let alone die, the experience of form includes the experience of fragility—and, for many, great suffering.

There's a perception that if something is an illusion, it can't be affected by the world or have an impact on the world. However, a desert mirage creates an illusion that can have serious consequences if you believe it to be actual water. It can lead you further into the dry, hot desert, away from safety. Declaring that your body is an illusion and almost entirely empty space while crawling through the scorching sand won't free you from pain and suffering, and neither will it prevent the death of the body.

If you don't see things as an illusion, how do you see them?

Rather than thinking of the material realm as an illusion, why not take the opportunity to experience the depth in everything? By "depth," we're referring to a deep quiet that's palpable, a stillness that's unaffected by the activity of your mind and body or the activity around you.

When we allow each moment to be as it is, it reveals its true nature beneath the surface representations we perceive. We discover that everything around us is more than what it appears to be. We quickly see that the expression "cold, harsh, light of reality" isn't true. Reality feels soft, welcoming, intimate, wondrous. Though very familiar, it's at the same time beautifully mysterious in a way that can't be sensed by the measuring and analyzing software of the mind.

When we are in touch with the depth dimension of reality, we feel relaxed, alert, and very accepting of the way life appears to be. As we enter the space that seemingly separates us from other people and other forms, it feels like a fullness instead of an emptiness.

In practical terms, if we walk into a large stadium full of people, on the surface there appears to be a vast, uncomfortable distance between everyone—an impenetrable void that causes people to feel alienated and disconnected from each other. But when we come from the deeper vantage point of awareness, it feels as if everyone in the stadium is very close and connected to us. When we believe ourselves to be a small, separate entity, our mind tries to guess what other people are thinking and whether they approve of us and can give us what we want. In our state of present moment awareness, we don't see enemies because we don't perceive a separate "other."

This sounds wonderful. But the present moment feels fleeting to me, insubstantial, and not very intimate.

When we fully inhabit the present moment, the deep stillness we experience possesses a "gravity" so strong that few thoughts or emotions can escape its pull, and mind content rapidly returns to the formlessness from which it came. With little to no mind content to contend with, we finally know the present moment to be the totality of existence—vast, eternal, and closer to us than our own beating heart.

Our egoic condition flips reality on its head, making our stories the totality of our existence. They feel very real and never-ending, superimposed over everything we experience. We are more intimate with our stories about people and the world than with what they actually are.

The present moment is all there is, although to most observers it appears as if reality is split up into countless individual pieces and isolated events. The deeper into the present moment we go, we notice that all of the individual forms, moments, and events of our lives are linked beneath the surface. Think of a chain of islands in an ocean that hides the fact they are merely the mountain peaks of a single submerged mountain range. In the act of stepping back to dissect, analyze, and reflect upon reality, the mind fails to recognize the present moment for what it actually is—the only experience there has ever been. The present is a single phenomenon, whole and indivisible, without beginning or end.

Living life in the present is a win-win situation. Regardless of what happens, the permanency of pure awareness empowers you and gives you a peaceful, clear-headed, and fearless foundation upon which to stand. You have the pleasure and honor of serving in the world of form to help alleviate personal and planetary suffering. None of this can happen without you. Your alert presence is the vehicle through which peace becomes manifest in this body, this world, and this universe.

PEACE IS YOUR RESPONSIBILITY

The peace that's already here will remain largely imperceptible until we each realize this peace for *ourselves*. The good news is that we have the ability to do so. Indeed, we have the response-*ability*. We don't have to change anyone else's beliefs or wait for legislation or peace accords to be signed in order to begin experiencing peace.

It's important to realize that the responsibility of allowing peace to arise in our daily circumstances is no more of a burden than noticing our breath is a burden. It's simply a matter of shifting our attention away from the abstract realm onto what's actual.

I run workshops and organizations that teach nonviolence. I have a nonprofit organization devoted to conflict resolution, and I have created booklets and websites with guidelines for nonviolence.

Anyone who is trying to make the world a better place by doing good works is actually seeking peace. All such efforts are noble and to be commended. We can be tremendously grateful for those who have the courage to take the kind of action that can bring about a better world. The degree to which a person's actions reflect how in touch they are with the peace within is the degree to which they will manifest peace in the world.

When our efforts don't make a lasting difference, often it's because our actions have more to do with the manufacturing of temporary conditions and little to do with the permanent peace this book is about. It's the difference between trying to "make" peace and entering into the peace that's already here. It's so easy for the false persona, in its efforts to "create" peace, to become a barrier to real peace. Indeed, it's the *only* barrier to the experience of peace.

But tell me, what are you referring to when *you* use the word "peace"?

It's when everyone and everything is quiet and relaxed. People are kind to each other and cooperative, which means everyone's happy and life is harmonious. There's no war, and the world's resources are shared equitably.

Many dream of the conditions you describe, yet they experience only brief periods of calm. Things improve for a time, but they don't stay that way. Couples, neighbors, and nations start arguing again. Eventually conflict, violence, and war break out afresh. This is why people say, "Nothing lasts forever."

However, *peace is eternal.*

To really know about peace is to embody the truth that you and peace are one. But since so many aren't aware of what they truly are, how can they possibly know lasting peace?

This lack of awareness is why, despite the efforts of activists, seekers, and indeed so many in the world who desire peace, an enduring peace escapes us.

Whether we are talking about domestic violence, poverty, destruction of the environment, or war, I believe education is the key to solving the world's problems.

When education flows from awareness, it indeed makes a difference. However, if it's coming purely from the head, the benefits it brings will always be limited. This is because for every "good" lesson learned, our ego can generate much more confusion, ignorance, and suffering. Also, education is a rather vague term. For instance, many have been conditioned to believe those born with a lighter skin are superior to those born with more melanin in their skin.

You might think that if people were just informed of the facts, things would change. However, smokers know the facts about smoking yet continue to harm themselves and others. Millions also know the facts about sedentary living and junk food, yet they don't change their ways, which is why hospitals are filled with patients with heart disease, organ failure, and many other illnesses related to poor nutrition and lack of exercise.

It isn't so much education that's needed, but for people to become realigned with the peace that's their essence. Every form, from atoms to people and planets, vibrates at a certain frequency. To return to our natural state is to realign ourselves with the primordial vibration that created all forms.

As the root vibration, peace-filled consciousness has the power to harmonize the many discordant energies in the universe and bring them back into alignment with it. Because the consciousness that fills space makes up almost the whole of every form, the vibration of permanent peace can rapidly return a form to alignment. Since at this higher level of consciousness time and space aren't a barrier, to embody peace is to resonate at a vibrational frequency that positively affects the entire universe.

We may feel better when peace replaces stress, but will that change our immediate circumstances? How does feeling peaceful prevent hunger or climate disaster?

The root of the problem is that the egoic self is in a constant state of "not enough," and therefore always on the lookout for the "next thing." Each ego seeks to adorn itself with more meaningful relationships, objects, and experiences in a futile attempt to feel whole and permanent.

The way the world works, one ego's success often depends on another ego failing to get what it wants. Because the ego's sense of self is partially derived from identifying with the forms it seeks to acquire, it feels diminished, its existence threatened, when denied what it desires.

Collectively, the ego produces an economic system in which obsessive consumption and hoarding are the norm. Competition, deception, and violence are the preferred methods of individuals and nations seeking to acquire more resources. The fact there are more than enough resources for everyone on the planet to live a happy, healthy, and struggle-free existence goes unnoticed. The ego can't help itself. Its paranoia perceives scarcity everywhere. This is the source of conflict in our world.

Many set out to act more peacefully, but this isn't the same as *being* peace. Though it's a good beginning, it's incomplete. When we recognize that we are all part of a single universal reality, our compulsive tendency to acquire more things by exploiting other forms disappears.

Also, when we are aware of our collective oneness, we no longer see other forms as a threat to our existence. Because we recognize them as other expressions of the same formless reality, we realize that to harm another is to harm ourselves.

The universal awareness that's our true being has an innate sense of equity and balance, which means it knows precisely what's necessary for the harmonious functioning of the whole. This harmonious state was perhaps more evident on our planet and in the universe for billions of years before the appearance of the human ego.

When humanity ceases to resist reality, the primordial intelligence can flow through us more easily and inform our thinking. Awakened from our dream of "me and my story," we now possess greater clarity, insight, and access to creative solutions to help us resolve humanity's most pressing issues, such as climate disaster. We actually feel a primordial urge to heal and unify, while respecting the uniqueness and inherent beauty of all forms.

Have you considered why you and your friends became activists, whereas so many others are largely indifferent?

Even in grade school some of the things we learned about the world seemed to affect me more than my classmates.

Everyone on the planet possesses a different level of consciousness. This is a measure of how aware we are of our collective oneness. Some seem to be born with greater awareness of our collective interdependence, while others may catch a glimpse of it in the presence of true peace, beauty, creativity, or something that evokes a sense of wonder.

However, many people are at a level of consciousness where they cannot sense their connection to a greater whole. This limits their capacity for empathy. When they express little to no concern for others outside of their family or social group, it's because they experience the world differently than you do. A sign of our own growing self-awareness is having empathy for those whose capacity for empathy is limited.

A glimpse of our oneness doesn't imply that the ego can directly view what is in fact beyond its capacity to perceive. The experience of oneness is the experience of reality without the filter of thought. It comes from our deepest being, not from thinking. After such an experience, thought can then reflect on it. But it can never create it.

Even though a glimpse of our oneness is quickly forgotten by many because they soon return to thought, this brief shift in consciousness can affect our level of empathy, compassion, and the way we live in the world. However, the mistake many of us make is to think we can make ourselves and others more conscious, and thereby change the world into a more peaceful place. The well-intentioned but thought-filled "me" is the impediment to the peace of higher consciousness.

In fact, all we can ever do is *allow the mysterious process of awakening to unfold.* Any conscious *doing* on our part is really an *allowing.* When we no longer resist reality, we allow a greater intelligence to inform our thoughts and actions. This higher intelligence can work through us but is beyond our thorough control or understanding. Through our presence we end our resistance. Peace re-emerges in us and becomes a greater possibility for others as well.

In the past, both online and on the frontline as an activist, I've used persuasive arguments backed by solid facts to change people's minds. Does this have a place in the natural process of unfolding awareness?

In this kind of interaction, one's level of consciousness is primary. Your level of awareness and the peaceful presence that accompanies it were far more important than any words you may have spoken. Note that a true change of mind goes beyond the mere holding of a new opinion. It involves a change of heart, which means a shift in empathy and a deeper understanding of how everything is connected.

It's one's level of consciousness—one's awareness of being part of the "whole"—that brings people a greater perspective on any issue. Those who are ready to hear and understand what you have to say do so because their level of consciousness is high enough to possess sufficient awareness of our interconnectedness. This fosters empathy and the ability to embrace a new perspective.

Devoid of presence, concepts can't create the greater understanding and empathy we long for others to experience. Our goal, then, is to increase the possibility of their consciousness rising by not impeding this natural process with our own egoic resistance to the present moment.

Like a cork floating up to the water's surface when a resisting hand is removed, our level of consciousness naturally rises when mental activity abates. This also increases the possibility that other people's consciousness may rise. When the level of a person's consciousness rises, their old narrative will begin to fall apart, sometimes subtly and sometimes dramatically. The person may now be ready for a narrative that better matches their new level of awareness.

When you talked with someone and they seemed to understand, you may have given them one final push over the edge to a new narrative that reflects the shift in consciousness we cannot perceive. Although they may believe the eloquence of your argument changed them, it's all a question of life having prepared a person for such a shift in consciousness. When we act with presence, we allow life to work through us. The increase in our own self-awareness helps us realize it isn't the egoic "me," but the compassionate intelligence of the one life, that does the "work" to raise consciousness.

Even if you didn't directly change a person's mind, helping people go where they are already headed is a good thing. The best way to do this is by offering no resistance to what *is*. Whether you remain silent or speak, anchoring yourself in the peace of the present moment is always the catalyst to increasing empathy, understanding, and awareness of peace.

To reiterate, resolving conflicts and educating about violence are worthy endeavors that can bring about positive yet temporary conditions of relative calm—temporary because the root of the problem goes unaddressed. The seeds of conflict and violence propagate as long as the dysfunctional mind remains in charge.

There will be no end to global suffering, no lasting peace, until we step away from the egoic trance that causes us to see each other as fundamentally separate from one another. Again, only when we recognize our intrinsic oneness will we realize we can never *have* peace and fulfillment, but can only *be* peace and fulfillment.

8

THE QUEST FOR JUSTICE

Many believe that when an injustice has occurred, before there can be peace, there must be justice. But is the call for justice truly a demand for things to be put right, which includes rehabilitation of the offender? Or does the reparation a victim seeks have more to do with a diminished ego that wishes to build itself up again? In other words, is it actually revenge that's being sought?

Saying that justice must come ahead of peace is to say that more suffering is required before we can allow peace. However, human history is evidence that suffering has never led to peace. Suffering only leads to further rounds of suffering.

The egoic condition severely restricts our compassion and empathy. We become highly selective in how we show generosity or caring, bestowing kindness on family, friends, or those individuals and groups we feel are worthy of it, while withholding from others and even showing hostility toward them.

Often all the ego needs to restore its diminished self is compensation in the form of a kind word, a gift, or a pleasurable activity. However, when the ego feels seriously victimized, positive compensation is considered inadequate, so it seeks punishment for the perpetrator.

As the ego takes offense and feels diminished, the pain-body takes us over. Now the suffering "me" gets its fill by taking pleasure in the pain of others. This is one of the reasons punishment and revenge have become the norm in the quest for justice.

Isn't punishment sometimes necessary, such as denying a perpetrator their freedom temporarily to protect society?

Short or long-term detainment to protect others and for the purpose of rehabilitation can be necessary and useful. However, notice that wherever egoic dysfunction, and therefore pain-body activity, increases on the planet, the call for "justice" often becomes code for revenge.

The cry for justice doesn't originate with the true self. This is because, once we realize we are one, we also realize our true self has never been diminished, hurt, or damaged. Remember, you are not your mind, your body, or your history.

The ego's demands for justice fade with the felt experience of our eternal oneness. When victims and perpetrators see through the veil of their ego-created identities, there will be no more victims or perpetrators. Each will recognize that, in their essence, the other is also an expression of peace, though they've temporarily lost sight of this. We'll all realize that those who harm others do so only because they are under the influence of a false self and don't truly know what they are doing.

Here is something you can do that will help you understand what real justice involves. Visualize the people toward whom you hold hostility. Notice how your body, especially the heart area, closes up. Now ask yourself, "Do I truly want peace for these individuals?"

Yes, I want them to be at peace. But if they were allowed to go unpunished, wouldn't they be getting away with something? If they are to learn not to harm others, surely there have to be consequences?

So you believe that more suffering leads to peace?

Also, who decides how much suffering is sufficient, other than the ravenous pain-bodies that always want more pain?

People who hurt others are already in pain themselves. Have you considered that their unconscious upbringing—with no sense of true peace and love—produced the unconscious, abusive behavior that followed in later years? The behavior of the physical body that commits injustice is always controlled by a dysfunctional ego that causes the individual to do hurtful things.

Responding with more suffering, especially when it's seen as a punishment, doesn't rehabilitate the individual. On the contrary, it threatens and diminishes the perpetrator's ego. Their ego learns it must manipulate, punish, and control others to rebuild its diminished state. This is why recidivism is so high. The person doesn't learn the lesson we want them to learn because suffering begets suffering.

Harsh punishment and revenge represent deeply unconscious behavior, which only begets more of the same. Further activating the pain-body that caused the dysfunction in the first place rarely results in the love, peace, wisdom, and clarity of higher consciousness.

What about an apology? Is that too much to ask?

The transformative and healing power of a heartfelt apology shouldn't be underestimated. However, many apologies are unsatisfactory because the perpetrator doesn't truly understand what they have done and therefore can't show the remorse hoped for.

There are stories of aboriginal communities in the past that were sufficiently evolved and courageous to use compassionate forms of restorative justice in even the most extreme cases. For example, a murderer might take the place of the victim in the victim's family. The family members would give the offender-turned-relative objects and garments of value and treat him or her like the sibling or child that was taken from them.[17]

---

[17] *Four Ways of Dealing with Murder among the Yankton Band of the Dakota Nation*, Living Justice Press, livingjusticepress.org

In such a situation, compassion opens the perpetrator's heart. The offender's dysfunctional state is gradually replaced by growing humility, respect, and love for their new family. Now there's a real opportunity for the offender to understand what they have done, which results in genuine remorse for the suffering they caused.

This approach worked when communities were small and everyone in the community was involved. Unfortunately, in the context of our present society, for a family to adopt a violent offender is unrealistic. Despite this, the principle involved continues to be valid. Responding with compassion is the best way to restore a measure of empathy in the perpetrator.

Empathy represents a higher level of consciousness that allows a perpetrator to perceive people and situations from more than their limited separate perspective. As the individual begins to sense the interconnectedness of all beings, they become capable of putting themselves in the other's shoes. The greater the empathy, the more deeply an offender is likely to feel and understand the suffering they have caused, which in turn discourages further offenses.

When I experience rage toward certain people, even my partner, I can't pretend to love them or wish them peace.

Anguish, and even rage, in reaction to a traumatic event are understandable. They can even be part of the healing process. However, long-term reactivity turns the initial upset into chronic suffering.

Let's step away from the matter of criminal justice for a moment and consider our personal relationship with a partner. During an argument with our partner, if we react too strongly to their behavior, our pain-body will become active, and we'll end up joining them in their miserable condition. It therefore behooves us to be aware that the offending ego's pain-body has the power to reactivate our own dormant pain-body to such an extent that, long after the event, we will be reacting to our own thoughts.

When we can't show compassion for a perpetrator, it isn't so much the individual we are denying love and peace. We are denying ourselves love and peace.

If you can't bear to be compassionate toward the offender, there's another way. Be compassionate with *yourself*. You have suffered enough. End your own suffering by returning to the present moment and the peace of your essential being.

Effortless *being* means you don't have to *do* anything, including forgiving the person. Instead, simply rest and bask in the love and peace you are. When you no longer come from your egoic self, you won't perceive this as a sacrifice on your part. Aligning with your formless nature allows peace and love to shine through, enabling you to see the other in a quite different light.

How will this help the situation?

It's only the ego that prevents us from feeling compassion toward others as well as ourselves. This false self resists any thought of compassion because it can't bear to project love or peace for fear it will be diminished if it does.

Since love and peace aren't something the ego can possess, this fear is unfounded. Although we talk about love and peace as something we can give and receive, in fact the false persona can do neither. Instead, when the ego disappears in the light of the present moment, we *become* love and peace.

Whereas continued anguish over the behavior of another helps neither ourselves nor anyone else, embodying peace not only heals us but gives us the strength to direct compassion to even the most violent offender. The powerful frequencies of peace and love from our source then resonate with the same essence deep within the offender. In this way, raising our level of consciousness makes it possible for the offender's to rise also, thereby increasing their capacity for empathy and compassion.

Healing is life's natural response whenever human egos recede. In this natural state of being, we no longer keep score of who needs to make amends and by how much. Paradoxically, reparations, apologies, and forgiveness often come quite spontaneously when we no longer demand them. This is because the ego isn't being triggered by our demands and therefore no longer impedes them with its resistance.

Showing compassion and equanimity during a traumatic event is only difficult if we haven't cultivated presence through the everyday events of our lives. People often wait until they are in crisis before they take steps to end the illusion of "me and my story." The result is that their progress toward greater clarity, equanimity, and compassion is slow.

In the heat of a crisis, there may be a buildup of energy in the body, which may be expressed as anger or fear. This is understandable and even helpful when there's a direct threat to the body. However, if we aren't practiced at moving into our peaceful center, this normal instinctual response may remain long after the threatening event has ended. It now turns into dysfunctional thinking and reactivity, which produces suffering.

Although it appears and feels as if what others have done produces our ongoing reactivity, in reality we are reacting to our own thoughts. As our interpretation of events produces strong emotions linked to our painful past, the pain-body re-emerges to pull us deeper into unconsciousness, moving us even further from the peace we are.

But am I just to stand aside if the person continues to create more suffering?

Take action if you must. But when you protect yourself or others from harm, do so with equanimity. Stay rooted in your peaceful center as you act, so that your actions are guided by a higher wisdom that knows the best way to respond to the situation.

To limit an aggressor's unconscious behavior, you yourself have to be alert and present, or you may get pulled into unconscious reactivity. Keep in mind that you aren't there to defend anyone's ego, including your own. When you avoid taking things personally, you lessen the likelihood of fueling the perpetrator's ego and pain-body, which would only cause them to intensify their aggression.

Realigning with the flow of life creates space for a new dynamic in which you no longer perceive the other as an opponent. Who knows what will happen then? You may end up peacefully yet firmly in their way. Or, with no one to oppose their ego, the person may simply capitulate.

In the many shootings that take place, it isn't my finger that pulls the trigger. Isn't the one who does the shooting to blame?

Blame contains a strong emotional component that promotes the idea we are all separate, all exclusively responsible for our actions. Recognizing how human society collectively creates perpetrators and victims is essential for true healing of our world to take place.

Because our egoic filter maintains the illusion of our separateness, it can be difficult for us to recognize our role in the creation of suffering. The false "me" seeks to attribute blame in situations it can't really understand.

The only difference between ourselves and the perpetrators of injustice lies in the degree of self-awareness and the uniqueness of our respective painful pasts. A perpetrator is someone who has crossed a threshold. Sometimes an individual only needs to feel sufficiently victimized to morph from an individual whose actions seem reasonable to one who commits crime or carries out acts of terror. Many of us teeter on the threshold, perhaps not in sufficient distress to become a perpetrator ourselves, but in enough pain to quietly condone or even cheer vengeful forms of punishment.

When someone does terrible things, it's because the unconsciousness of society—which includes the family of the accused, teachers, communities, governments, and each of us—created a child who became an unconscious adult. Each generation's unconsciousness can be linked to the previous generation, which taught their children from the same unaware state, all the way back to the beginning of our species. No single individual human or group is to blame for this inherent unconsciousness, but each of us is responsible for freeing ourselves from our mental prisons.

Compassionate approaches to justice seek to meet the needs of victims, offenders, and the entire community. These alternatives to punishment expand our focus beyond the criminal act, to include social conditions and relationships. Such alternatives reflect our growing awareness of our interdependence and collective oneness.

"Responsibility" has a dual meaning. We all have a role in the current unconsciousness of humanity. As we become more aware, we also have the *ability to respond* and end this unconsciousness and the suffering it produces. Awareness of our true nature leads to empathy, compassion, and conscious behavior that can prevent further unconscious behavior. Blaming another without recognizing our role is not conscious behavior. Higher consciousness means we experience greater awareness of our interdependence, interconnectivity, and ultimate oneness. Knowing we are essentially one in peace ends the suffering and ignorance that lead to the harming of others.

The problem is that most don't know this, including those accused of injustice. The vast majority simply have no idea yet that recognizing our true nature is the key to preventing cruel, selfish people from emerging in the first place. If they knew better, they would do better. This is why we forgive.

I am reminded of the quote, "We have met the enemy and he is us."[18]

The humbling implication that we must look at ourselves in order to see the source of injustice of every kind makes this quote insightful. However, it's best not to think of the ego as an enemy. To perceive anyone or anything as an enemy is a state of resistance and often leads to reactivity that pulls us deeper into unconsciousness.

Once we realize we are a single universal consciousness interacting with itself, we see why it's wise not to take things too personally. Any

---

[18] Kelly, Walt. *Pogo*, Post-Hall Syndicate, 1971.

fear or anger on our part can't transform people who don't recognize our ultimate oneness. On the contrary, it serves only to strengthen their ego.

The more present, relaxed, and alert we are, the less likely we are to react to the ego's distorted and incomplete interpretation of reality. To keep yourself anchored in the present moment, make use of inner body awareness, feeling the vibrant aliveness that's always there. Maintaining a quiet mind and open heart then becomes the catalyst for the emergence of empathy within others. At the very least, a hostile situation is less likely to spiral out of control.

To remain egoless is no small challenge in a world in which billions of ego-driven pain-bodies seek to feed on the reactions of others—a world in which the social classes, religions, corporations, governments, and even rights organizations mistake each other as adversaries, when in fact they all suffer from the same affliction.

Consider the fact that the news and entertainment industries survive by capturing the attention of as many people as possible. Playing on our desires and fears, they sensationalize, encourage us to fantasize, and at their worst, promote division and the sense that others are "against" us. Since advertising dollars are based on the number of viewers, readers, and listeners, these businesses need us to become their captive audience. They have perfected the art of grabbing our attention for profit and thrive on promoting argument, hostility, and division. Everything from billboards and magazines to videos and text messages keep us wanting, distracted, and trapped in the virtual realm of the mind and its supposed "enemies."

Having said this, don't now turn politicians and pundits into enemies too. The media clips and sound bites for which these individuals are responsible are but fractions of their own lives. These people eat, sleep, put on socks, and so on, just like you. If you saw them in person, you'd see the mundane and typical behavior of any human. Remember, they are under the spell of unconsciousness and therefore unaware of what they are doing. By reacting to their false persona, you too come under the spell. If you cannot stay rooted in peace, how can you expect others who have no awareness of their true nature to do so?

See through their disguise, and before reacting consider that if you are peace, they are peace also.

Does this include the most hateful person I can think of?

Yes, it includes even the person you perceive to be your worst "enemy," and even the most hated person on earth.

To "love your enemies," simply recognize there's no completely separate other, and you will have no enemies.[19] Return to the reality of the present moment, where you'll recognize the truth of our ultimate oneness.

To love people doesn't mean we have to approve of their actions. But neither do we need to disapprove, since this would be to resist what *is*. Simply rest in a state of awareness, and watch the illusion of an "enemy" disappear. Peace and love will be all that remain when the illusion ends.

Because the road back home to our original peaceful nature lies in our ability to discern the real versus the virtual, deep body awareness is essential in the quest for personal and global peace. Each of us must experience this for ourselves. Inhabiting the present moment through body awareness is the responsibility of every individual.

Although achieving world peace by each becoming an expression of peace may seem daunting, the reality is that it's only a matter of letting go of our resistance to what *is*. When we do so, we quickly realize how empowering it is to fully feel our bodies and experience life without the "fear and division filter" of the ego.

Feeling your body is the most radical and revolutionary act this world may ever know. Indeed, there is no greater threat to the current egoic world order that produces violence, inequality, and suffering on a massive scale. Turn away from the virtual realm of thought, and watch humanity's selfish power structures tremble. Watch their foundations crumble because you no longer play the collective ego's game of "not one, not peace."

---

[19] Tolle, Eckhart. *The Power of Now,* Namaste Publishing, 1997, p. 171.

Your attention is your consent. The game of separation, division, and fear cannot continue without your attention fixed on it. You and the rest of humanity can continue to be victims, or we can together become the heroes who save the world. All we have to do to be truly heroic is feel the body and return to the sanity and reality of the peace of the present moment.

9

WHAT TO DO IF YOU'RE SICK OF SUFFERING

A re you tired of all this talk about peace? Don't you simply want to be at peace?

Yes, I'm sick of suffering, I just want it to stop.

Notice that the "I" that's sick of suffering is also the one generating the suffering. This is why who you *think* you are can't stop it. You haven't become sick of your identity yet, but are still so fascinated with your own personal story that you also want everyone else to be enchanted by it.

If you want action, there are active steps you can take to undo the abstract realm of thought in which you've become entangled. These steps aren't a new philosophy to memorize and decide whether it will replace your old bundle of beliefs. They are a roadmap that will enable you to stop analyzing and turn your attention to the present moment. The only permanent solution is to turn away from our hypnotic personal narratives and come to rest in the present moment.

Turning our attention to the reality of the uninterpreted moment brings a whole new meaning to the phrase "rest in peace." We realize we can be engaged in vigorous activity and yet be completely at rest inside, since we offer no resistance to the flow of life. It's our resistance that's so tiring. Waiting until the end of life to rest in peace means we have failed to experience the primary purpose of our existence, since we were born to live life in a state of complete ease. As we experience the peace at our core, we live all of life passionately.

When we aren't at rest, our life could be likened to a clenched fist. If we now unclench our fist, the ego might interpret this as having worked to become relaxed. This act would seem quite impressive if we didn't know that our fist is simply returning to its natural state. In a clenched state, we are resisting what *is*. Accessing peace means we stop resisting, which is as simple as unclenching our fist. When we cease the act of clenching, our fist spontaneously enters into its naturally restful state.

The ego stays in control by operating unobserved and thus uncontested during much of each day. Becoming present and alert enough to notice when we're thinking is therefore an important step in our evolution. We notice the voice in our head that pretends to be us and almost never stops talking. The more frequently we interrupt the reverie of "me" with present moment awareness, the greater the number of gaps that develop in our false sense of self.

As "the story of me" dissolves, awareness of a peace-filled intelligence and clarity emerges. At first we simply take refuge in the soothing calm that accompanies present moment awareness. Eventually we recognize this peace as "home," our very essence.

What do you have to give up in order to live as peace?

Nothing. There isn't one part of your life that you have to give up in order to end your suffering. Live, play, and work in the house, community, or country of your choosing. Take the bus, a bicycle, or a Mercedes-Benz, it doesn't matter. Wear homemade clothing or high-fashion, it makes no difference. Work as a scientist, pop star, or gardener, whatever you choose.

The end of the ego doesn't mean the end of all personality traits, only that we have no attachment to them because they aren't who we are. Negative traits and dysfunctional behavior will gradually disappear because they reflect a resistance that's coming to an end. The most authentic and positive parts of our personality remain and may include our particular sense of humor, sense of style, and the unique way we express ourselves and view the world. In addition, we will likely find that any special gifts or skills are enhanced when compulsive thought and emotional reactivity disappear.

To the mind, it appears a life of peace is a life of aloofness and detachment—a life without passion. Quite the opposite, conscious living is passionate living. The reality is that a large number of people on the planet are "the walking dead," people with little passion. They keep to themselves, unless they happen to agree with someone, appear somewhat like each other, or have something they want from each other. The planet in general lives without passion, for which people substitute an intensity, neediness, and emotional volatility that has little to do with true passion.

We can look to nature and the universe and its passionate celebration of existence. There's nothing boring about a volcano, a thunderstorm, or the beautiful, explosive colors from star and galaxy formation. Standing in a jungle clearing as a flock of parrots flies overhead, or in a field of flowers that are blooming before our eyes, how can we not see that the source from which everything springs knows all about passion. As an expression of this source, we are passion itself. In contrast, the ego that pretends to be who we are is the very definition of dullness, desperation, and detachment.

When we awaken to our true nature, we also feel the joy of being. Boredom can't exist in the presence of joy. We finally begin to live with passion, even if it's not always expressed overtly.

Living creatively comes naturally, and it isn't important in which field or discipline we do this. It isn't so much what we do, but how we do it that matters. Whether you are a plumber, a nurse, or an artist, it's the quality of your awareness that counts. You can keep your relationships, your house, your career, and your favorite hobbies and pastimes, or you can acquire new ones. But now you engage in them fully and completely like never before, effortlessly and free of stress.

My husband operates a construction crane and I take care of three kids at home. We need to be very alert. We can't be floating around in blissful peace all the time.

People have a tendency to assume that constant thinking is required for alertness and practical living, whereas incessant thinking actually reduces our alertness, rendering us much less efficient as we perform our various tasks. Alertness without relaxation is similar to the "fight, flight, or freeze" state associated with tension and fear. Chronic use of this survival mentality results in stress that reduces clarity and alertness. True alertness and mental clarity originate from deep relaxation and a quiet mind.

One of the barriers to living more consciously is the lack of trust the ego has in a deeper intelligence to handle practical, day-to-day affairs. Conscious eating, conscious relationships, or consciously performing any activity is about trusting life to take the helm whenever we are engaged in the practical matters of day-to-day living. Surrendered to what *is*, we realize that the peace-filled intelligence that created the body knows how to guide it effortlessly through any task, relationship, or experience.

Who knows what secrets the body may reveal when our relationship to it is no longer that of egoic master and servant? Or, said differently, bully and bullied. Even the mind becomes more efficient when used deliberately and less frequently. Primordial intelligence can flow into our thoughts, providing us with the insights and wisdom necessary for an optimal response to any situation.

So you're not talking about living in some kind of altered state?

Many tend to equate living peacefully with some sort of blissed-out altered state. The truth is, the vast majority are already living in an altered state produced by incessant thinking and reacting.

The voice in the head that pretends to be who we are creates a distorted picture of reality. Overreacting to situations and making erroneous assumptions about other people and their ways of living are typical for the average person. Indeed, living through the filter of the false self is the very definition of living in an altered state. This is why waking up out of our dream of "me" and returning to our natural state of presence and the peace that accompanies it is the most practical thing we can ever do.

Just in case you are wondering what will motivate you to help others, or to do anything for that matter, our naturally relaxed and peaceful state is also a state in which we are spontaneously creative. However, this creativity springs from a very different source than the "drivenness" of the ego, which acts out of a sense of lack.

Since the source of everything is completely fulfilled in itself, what motivation does it have to create anything? And yet it does create, constantly and effortlessly. It creates not from an air of desperation, but with a spirit of celebration. The extraordinary number and variety of species and objects in the universe weren't created because each and every one is essential for the continuation of existence, but solely for the joy of it.

When we experience creativity, it carries the higher frequency of *being*. Something literally resonates within us when we are inspired by creative expression. Even the vibrational frequency of our body rises. In that moment of grace, the musician becomes the music, the dancer becomes the dance, and the scientist is one with the formula or equation.

When we awaken to our true nature, love, flowing out of a state of peace, motivates us to meet needs and help wherever we can. Joy and beauty inspire us to create, express ourselves, and inspire others.

THE ANTIDOTE TO ADDICTION

E go is essentially addiction to thought. Thinking is the original addictive pattern from which all other addictions are born.

The simple act of engaging the mind creates resistance, which feels like psychological and physical pressure. As a result, the ego seeks out satisfying objects and experiences to relieve this pressure, unaware that its very existence creates more resistance. Because some things temporarily relieve this discomfort, the ego turns to them again and again. The compulsive thinker unavoidably creates compulsive emotional and physical habits, but their ability to comfort us provides diminishing returns.

All relationships with food, alcohol, people, technology, and so on lose their compulsive quality when the ego loses its grip on us under the impact of present moment awareness.

I like to tell myself my eating habits are a celebration of life. But there's a hint of desperation in my attempts to feel full.

This isn't uncommon. Food is just one way the ego tries to eliminate its sense of inadequacy. Whether what's in front of us is food, a romantic partner, or a mobile phone, if we remain lost in the abstract realm of thought, the person or activity that brings us pleasure today will be mistaken for the cause of our frustration and pain tomorrow. As long as we behave as if forms are the key to fulfillment, the endless cycle of hurt, disappointment, and abuse continues.

In contrast, when our attention is fully on the present moment, we don't require food, a person, or a text message to fulfill us. The fulfillment of simply *being* is enough, with or without the forms we seek. As the embodiment of peace and contentment, we are then free to enjoy the food, person, or technology in front of us. We may also discover the intensity of our wanting has prevented us from fully experiencing the food, people, and activities we are drawn to. It's as if we were tasting something, or truly understanding and connecting with someone, for the first time.

Regularly becoming aware of our body and breath throughout the day means that the psychological and physical compulsion for "more" can't build up, since attending to the body creates space sufficient to dissipate any pressure. In this state of ease, we're less likely to feel strong cravings for particular experiences, things, or people.

As the pressure to acquire and consume lessens, we enjoy a growing desire to simply experience whatever comes into contact with our senses. For example, eating becomes a fascinating activity when we no longer engage in it mindlessly or with feelings of guilt.

When eating becomes more of a journey than a goal, the focus of our attention—the food, plate, or table—is met with a softened gaze. We notice that performing any action slowly, deliberately, and with alert awareness prevents the mind from going into autopilot. We inhale slowly and deeply the aromas of what we've chosen to become one with. We feel the temperature and texture of the fork as it gently deposits food in our mouth. We feel the weight and texture of the food, as well as enjoy the complexity of flavors as the food rests on our tongue. Taking a full breath, we turn our attention inward, closing our eyes if necessary, to observe the sensation of chewing and swallowing. During the entire activity, we notice our breathing, keeping our muscles relaxed, feeling the aliveness within our body.

Giving our full attention to any experience is quite different from focusing on the judgments and reactions we have concerning the experience. The important thing is to allow the experience to unfold with as quiet a mind as possible. When our attention isn't absorbed by mental chatter—the "play-by-play commentary" on what's happening—it naturally comes to rest in the present moment.

Isn't addiction largely a biochemical issue?

When there's a biochemical component to addiction, it can't survive too long without the physical and psychological pressure that arises from resisting what *is*. Compulsion and unnatural craving in the body can't continue without the egoic mind that incessantly thinks and constantly wants more.

In the case of an addiction to food, a feeling of hunger tells us when it's time to nourish the body, but the compulsive voice in the head distorts the body's natural signals, thereby creating pangs of hunger far in excess of our basic physical needs.

The ego is concerned with trying to fulfill its sense of "me" and uses the body to accomplish this. The body's hunger for food, entertainment, power, sex, alcohol, and so on, masks its deeper desire for attention from our essential being. Our attention not only creates the space that dissipates physical pressure and craving, but also quiets the ego that's the source of all compulsions and addictions. Bringing our attention into the present moment is the antidote to all compulsive activity of mind and body.

It's okay to want things without being addicted to them, right?

The ego operates exclusively in the realm of material forms and considers itself an expert in this domain. But have you ever truly reflected on why you do some of the things you do? For instance, why do you really want a particular car, job, house, or relationship? Do you even know why you want a glass of water, watch TV, or feel the texture of a tree leaf?

You might reply, "Simple. I want water when I'm thirsty, I watch TV to relax and unwind, and I touch objects I've never touched before because I'm curious."

It certainly sounds simple, until you ask a further question. If satisfying your thirst, relaxing, or being curious made you feel bad, would you do these things? Most likely you'd look for something else to satisfy your needs and wants. But why do you even wish to satisfy your needs and wants?

If you answer, "Because if I satisfy my needs and wants, I'll feel good," then also answer this further question: "Why does satisfying needs and wants feel good?"

On the surface, we may be motivated by the quest for wealth, power, or celebrity. However, if you look closely, you'll find there's an *underlying* need, which is for security, control, and approval. Even when a job brings us self-esteem and a relationship brings us love, we're really trying to satisfy a still deeper drive.

Behind all of these form-based needs and wants is the ultimate need, the primordial desire to feel good. Quenching our thirst feels good. Security and approval feel good. Love feels good. Even curiosity—the wonder, excitement, and satisfaction that come from learning or experiencing something new—feels good. But why do we want to feel good?

We want to feel good *because we want to feel God.*

In other words, we want to feel good in order to experience who we really are. Love, joy, and peace feel good because they are goodness itself. It's because *we* are primordial goodness that we enjoy feeling good.

Although it isn't apparent to the thinking mind, the reason we do anything is out of a desire to return to the natural sense of wellbeing that comes from being aligned with the flow of life. To align with life is to be one with it. It's to realize that we are the love, joy, and peace of ultimate *being*, which emerges when we no longer resist what *is*.

Life coaxes us into returning home to our true self by making certain experiences feel good and others bad. Of course, the ego is unaware that our desire to feel good contains the deeper desire to return to our essential being. Nevertheless, we are programmed to experience peace sooner or later because we are hardwired for paradise. This is what makes life a win-win situation.

The ego wants to exist forever, yet it doesn't realize that it's the impediment to *being,* which alone is eternal.

When we come from ego, we hold the subconscious belief that somewhere "out there" are forms that can bring us what we really want, such as fulfillment, wholeness, and immortality. The ego is restricted by its very nature to search the form-based universe for the wholeness, goodness, and Godness it craves. However, the forms we desire can never bring us the experience of that which is formless.

God is formless—no beard, no sandals, no body. Consequently, the fulfillment and permanence characteristic of peace are experienced only when we are in touch with our formless nature.

Eckhart Tolle articulates a great truth when he writes, "God-realization is the most natural thing there is. The amazing and incomprehensible fact is not that you can become conscious of God but that you are not conscious of God."[20]

I just realized what you mean. Feeling good is the motivation beneath every surface desire, since the desire to feel God is behind all surface desires.

How could it be otherwise? God is behind everything, the source of all forms and experiences. Everything we perceive is simply God expressed in some form or other.

There is *only* God.

Good, in the absolute sense, is the same as God. For this reason, when we tell ourselves we are *not* good, we're also playing the game of "not experiencing God." But this game is no longer fun for most of us. Living on the surface of reality, we're unaware of the primordial goodness of our essential being. In fact, we may even suspect we're bad.

Although operating from the false persona causes us to act

[20] Tolle, Eckhart. *The Power of Now,* Namaste Publishing, 1997, p. 189.

unconsciously, which produces suffering for ourselves and others, this doesn't make us bad. Rather, it means we are under a spell and therefore unaware of what we are doing. We aren't "bad," just lost and in need of help to find our way home to our original being.

Doesn't it come as a huge relief to know that goodness, which is the essence of Godness, is behind everything—especially when you think you've blown it and feel really bad about yourself?

Since nothing but God exists, to seek ourselves is to seek God. To seek enjoyment in anything is to seek God.

It's strange to think that when I go to the kitchen for something tasty, I'm actually searching for God.

Since everything around us is temporary and subject to dissolution at any moment, nothing in the material realm can ever truly satisfy. If we wish to feel good on a consistent basis, the only permanent and truly fulfilling good is to be found in pure being.

Although desires and goals pursued by the ego can never provide complete fulfillment, when we bring our deeper being to our relationships, acquisitions, and aspirations, they become fulfilling. They are fulfilling because *we* are fulfilled, and we bring this inner state to our experiences. The material realm then becomes a means of expressing and celebrating how terrific we feel inside ourselves.

It's the fact we are fulfilled beings *in and of ourselves,* quite apart from anything material, that makes our family, possessions, pursuits, and dreams important to us. To the degree we bring our essential wholeness to these forms in each moment of the present, we experience them as satisfying.

Whereas coming from pure being makes everything meaningful, inviting us to invest deeply in each aspect of our lives, attachment to any form in the hope it can bring us satisfaction leads only to endless dissatisfaction. Feeling dissatisfied, we may then even neglect the very people, things, and pursuits that have the potential to be intensely pleasurable.

Whenever we crave something, it appears that the object of our desire is separate from us. In other words, we perceive it as *something we don't have.* We think of it existing across an empty space that lies between us and itself, and this illusion of a distance between us triggers the feeling of craving.

Craving is the opposite of enjoying. It arises because we don't recognize that the object of our desire isn't separate from us but is already one with us. The apparent empty space between us is simply the ego's inability to perceive our essential oneness. Once we realize this, we see the Godness in the space, which turns out to be not an emptiness but a fullness.

The space that makes up the majority of most forms, as well as what's between us, is full of peace, joy, wisdom, love, and creative potential. These fundamental characteristics of being are formless "no-thing." Unable to perceive the overflowing fullness within formlessness, the ego misinterprets empty space as a feeling of lack *inside* of us and as the reason for the experience of separation *outside* of us.

As we recognize the fullness in ourselves, as well as in the space between ourselves and the object of our craving, to be our own Godness, this recognition quiets the mind, returning us to a state of peace and a sense of the goodness and completeness of life. Coming from the fullness of Godness, our craving and neediness disappear.

Free of craving, we're now free to enjoy everything in the material realm to whatever degree it makes itself available to us—without having to latch onto it to try to fill a supposed emptiness or lack within us, which is just a mirage of the ego.

So although we can't ever "have it all," we can *be* it all.

Who knew that salvation lies in the space between the sofa and the fridge!

Yes, the answer to personal and world peace is between the sofa and the fridge—or for that matter, between any two forms. The forgettable and nearly imperceptible space between where we think we are and what we want holds the key to personal and global peace and enlightenment, since when we make space in our lives for space itself, there's nothing "separate" to which the ego can relate or attach itself.

Wherever we are, we can make it a habit to notice the physical volume of the place we're in, in which the amount of visible space far exceeds the quantity of any forms. Then, while feeling the aliveness within our body, if we soften our gaze and notice the empty space between ourselves and whatever we are currently looking at, we will become aware of the totally satisfying peace and fullness within us and everywhere.

As long as we stay rooted in the present moment through body awareness, this one continuous moment contains everything we ever wanted. We experience peace and joy each step of the journey, which causes any physical destination or form-based desire to no longer seem so important.

Relieved of the burden that our loved ones, possessions, or dreams must fulfill us, they can simply be enjoyed for however long they are in our life.

Recognize you are an expression of the All, the formless source hidden in all forms, and you are finally free. You can experience the love, joy, fulfillment, sense of permanence, and immortality you've long sought.

THE END OF WAITING

For many of us, the space between where we are and where we wish to be is a frustrating nuisance. Our psychological need for the next moment makes us impatient, so that we fail to value the here and now. We treat this moment as a means to an end—or, worse, as an obstacle to fulfillment.[21]

A conscious life is lived in the present, where we realize that experiencing the reality of this moment is the only way to know fulfillment. We end our resistance to what *is* and accept things as they are.

On the surface of reality, our bodies may be physically waiting for another person or event to cross our path before we can have what we want. However, in our deeper being, there is no sense of expectancy for anyone or anything. We are simply here, completely at ease with the moment unfolding in whatever way it does.

I wait all day in traffic, at ATMs, in the checkout line, for other people—the list goes on.

Your body may need to wait for one event to be followed by another. But does an attitude of negativity toward waiting help in any way? In fact, does your mind need to be engaged during the time your body is waiting?

---

[21] Tolle, Eckhart. *A New Earth,* Dutton, 2005, p. 202.

Notice that any impatience or frustration that accompanies the simple act of being where you are serves no useful purpose. For instance, when you feel inconvenienced, complaining to yourself doesn't magically change the reality of the situation. Glaring at the cashier doesn't speed up the line. Cursing under your breath doesn't get you what you want any sooner.

We behave as if a deity or other powerful force will be compelled to clear the obstacles in our path if we just express enough resentment. In reality, all we're doing is reinforcing the false sense of "me," which means we're pulled more deeply into the virtual realm of thought.

Although it appears the *situation* is creating discomfort, it's actually our interpretation of what's happening that causes our unease. We react negatively because the egoic condition is one of dissatisfaction and fear. Our mental filter—made compulsive and dysfunctional by identifying with it—prevents us from perceiving things as they truly are. The egoic voice that judges and complains is normal but not natural, and neither is the unease and suffering it produces.

Whether our ego feels "pleased" or "wronged" is largely irrelevant. Its goal is survival, and any experience, "positive" or "negative," suffices to keep the mind engaged. The fact that it's constantly operating keeps us out of the reality of the present moment.

Many feel they don't have time to add techniques and practices to their busy day, and yet they complain about how many minutes or even hours they regularly spend waiting. Why not turn this time into a spiritual practice? All of this free time furnishes an opportunity to cultivate present moment awareness throughout the day, especially in those areas of life in which the ego is dominant, such as family, work, and leisure.

Here are some suggestions. Mute the television during commercials and feel the temperature of your breath as you inhale and exhale. Unclench your jaw, shoulders, and solar plexus and diaphragm while waiting for a web page to load or a reply to your text message. Fully feel the clothing and objects in contact with your body while you wait in line, in traffic, or for an appointment. Feeling the impact in your thighs as you walk is more important than the destination you are fixed on.

Whenever you catch yourself "waiting," go limp, leaving only essential muscles engaged, turning your attention inward to physically sense your body and breathing.

Returning our attention frequently to the reality of the present moment creates gaps in the thought stream that contains our personal narrative, our story of "me." The result is a significant reduction in the pressure and discomfort that arises from the ego's resistance to this moment. Eventually, we will be able to stay anchored in the body during any activity, waiting or not. By keeping part of our awareness on the feeling of aliveness within the body, our need for the next moment dissolves.

Sometimes my frustration isn't really about waiting in line.
It's the feeling that I'm waiting for my life to begin.

This is the case for almost everyone at some point. We *are* in a sense "waiting for life to begin." Or rather, we are waiting for the experience of our *true* life to begin.

The reason we sense something is missing from our life is that the ego, which is incapable of truly perceiving the here and now, is convinced its fulfillment lies somewhere in the future. It mistakenly believes life will begin with the acquisition of new and better things, when in fact it begins the moment we enter the present moment.

Life can only begin when the "story of me" ends—when the egoic impediment is dissolved.

Although our egoic condition pulls us out of alignment with the flow of life, we haven't been abandoned. Life is designed to pull us back to reality. It instills in us the desire to feel good and sends out a signal of discomfort and pressure to guide us back to our natural state of being.

You may object that most people aren't getting the message. It's true the egoic condition of our planet has become so extreme that most don't pick up on life's signals during their lifetime. However, this situation is beginning to change. Millions are becoming aware that the experience of their true nature is within their grasp while they are physically alive.

We can also take comfort in the knowledge that life goes on, so that not even death of the body can prevent us from discovering the truth of who we are.

I think my disappointment and dissatisfaction stem from knowing deep inside that there's more to life. It has to be better than this.

If you could experience things as they truly are—experience just *this*, right now—fulfillment would replace your dissatisfaction and, as happened with me, your searching would come to an end.

The expectation that life should be other than what it is, and that we ourselves should be different, comes largely from the ego's sense of incompleteness and compulsive orientation toward the future. All around us, life carries a signature of authenticity and reality that contrasts sharply with our abstract, mind-derived sense of "me."

Every now and then life's signals penetrate our egoic resistance and we sense our inauthenticity. Since the ego is an imposter, we actually feel phony at times. This is part of life's design to coax us back home to the wholeness of our inherent oneness. It can be traced back to the blueprint each of us carries within ourselves.

What appears to us as empty space is filled with a silent intelligence that contains the code for higher consciousness, which is awareness of our divine nature. This formless awareness is quietly working away in the background to remind us of who we are. Remember, our constant quest to feel good is ultimately the desire to experience God.

This is why anything that makes us feel good for a while leaves us with a sense that this temporary feeling of goodness is only the tip of the iceberg. As you put it, we realize there "has to be more." Encoded into everything we seek is the subtle sense of what we can be, which is the realization of what we really are—permanent peace and goodness.

If feeling good is part of life's plan, then it's okay to have expectations, isn't it?

Expectations are a form of waiting, and as such they carry a certain amount of dissatisfaction with the present moment. So, it's certainly okay to have expectations if you don't mind suffering! However, life's plan is for us to pay attention to the signals of discomfort and suffering, recognizing that they come from being lost in the abstract realm of thought.

Although expectations involve attachment to the future, and are therefore an indication we're saying "no" to reality as it is, there's nothing wrong with being hopeful or enthusiastic about future possibilities. We can have preferences for certain outcomes without being attached to them. It's when our preferences become expectations that we resist the flow of life. We wind up trying to fulfill the endless needs and wants of our ego instead of experiencing fulfillment here and now.

Up until now, the basic sensations of discomfort and pleasure have had limited success in pointing us in the right direction. However, some of life's signals are more effective than others. For instance, whenever we feel inspired by someone or something, it's as if life has finally plucked the right string for us to resonate with, which is of course different for each person. Some of us resonate with the words of a teacher, while others find words less inspiring than an act of compassion. Still others may be inspired by the creativity and beauty expressed in nature or a work of art. Whatever we are drawn to is an opportunity to see and feel the divine essence within that form—in other words, to catch a glimpse of our true self.

However, it can be a long wait between flashes of inspiration. So in order to experience reality more frequently, it helps to go into the body. We have seen that compulsive craving and impatient waiting are symptoms of a dysfunctional mind, eliciting physical and psychological pressure that dulls our felt awareness of the body and its energy field. By simply turning our attention to the body to experience its sensations and vitality, we can reduce the pressure and unease that would otherwise turn into greater suffering.

Just as we become better runners by running, and better feelers by feeling, consistently experiencing physical sensations without interpreting them restores our body sensitivity. The deeper we go into the body to feel its energy field and the stillness beneath, the deeper is our experience of the present moment.

12

HOW TO LIVE CONSCIOUSLY

M any seekers are hoping for the "big moment," when they are dramatically thrust into the depths of being like Eckhart Tolle was. However, this form of awakening is a rare experience. It's more likely enlightenment will come gradually, as a result of cultivating presence.

Thankfully, in order for us to benefit from breath and body awareness, a permanent shift in consciousness isn't required. When we inhabit our body, even small improvements in present moment awareness can significantly reduce stress and suffering.

We begin by maintaining our awareness of surface physical sensations. Keeping our attention on bodily sensations and movements gradually enables us to go deeper and perceive a subtle energy that flows through all forms, including our body. The longer we remain anchored in this vital energy, the easier it is to follow it back to its source—eternal stillness. Essence, or being, is a primordial peacefulness and stillness that paradoxically is also vibrantly alive.

Think back to our earlier discussion of breathing. When was the last time you noticed your breathing? Since then, have you made a point of feeling cool air moving through your nostrils, throat, and upper lungs as you inhale? How about the warmer air in these three areas as you exhale? Take a moment now to feel the difference in temperature between your inhale and your exhale.

Along with noticing your breathing, have you also been practicing feeling your body? For instance, have you tried unclenching any body parts that are unnecessarily tense, such as your jaw, shoulders, or solar plexus? Take a moment to notice and feel the clothing and objects that are in contact with your body. These may include accessories, a chair, the floor, and anything in your hands.

I forgot to follow the guidance given earlier, so this is the first time I've noticed my breathing and truly felt my body in quite a while.

When you are learning to live consciously, it's best to return to the here and now frequently. For example, you can try noticing the sensation of breathing after the answer to each question you read, and you can add the practice of feeling your body and unclenching your muscles at the end of each chapter. Don't just go through the motions. Become very still, switching off, and go within to immerse yourself in the sensory world of your body.

After a few attempts at this, the mind may try to convince you this practice is better left for some other time and place. However, cultivating awareness can't wait for the meditation cushion or the yoga mat, since the tendency is for it to become confined to these. Rather, a wise person cultivates awareness in each and every moment, since no other place or time is real.

As useful as traditional awareness practices are to reduce stress and increase self-awareness, for most people these sessions are brief and periodic. If we are to dislodge the ego from its position of power, we must bring the light of our consciousness into the most mundane tasks and everyday activities. We must do this consistently all day, even if only for a few seconds at a time. Since the ego considers most areas of our lives, such as family, friends, work, play, food, clothing, and shelter, as its exclusive domain, the more frequently we bring present moment awareness to these everyday relationships and activities, the more we will trust our inner being to run our life instead of relying on the ego.

To breathe consciously is to be alert enough to feel the physical sensation of breathing. To live consciously is to perform our daily activities and meet each situation with a quiet mind. We approach each task and situation with an "ease, grace, and lightness of being,"[22] unconcerned with the "what ifs" of the past or future because something needs our attention right now. We are aware that what needs our attention the most is the present moment. We use our awareness of body and breath to keep our attention anchored here in the real, free of mental distraction and emotional reactivity.

My mantras and visualizations calm me down. Isn't that good?

While it's true that there are practices that can provide a measure of short-term relief, knowing yourself as peace will likely continue to elude you because these practices typically keep the mind engaged. When emphasis is placed on an external practice, conscious living can rapidly devolve into a pseudo spiritual lifestyle.

It's also the case that the egoic mind's fear of dissolution encourages it to select teachings and practices that are less of a threat to its existence. After all, why merely feel your breath when you can think happy thoughts or say a mantra instead?

Practices that keep us lost in the abstract realm of thought and imagination can't create the conditions for a permanent shift in consciousness. The power of any technique lies in our felt experience while performing it. For example, if we focus on the vibrations rippling through our body during our mantras, we give new life and potency to a practice the egoic mind has largely neutralized.

Our felt experience of the uninterpreted moment is always more important than the yoga or meditation posture we hold, the clothing we wear, the books we read, and the group or teacher we are a disciple of. Looking and superficially acting like a conscious person makes the ego feel good for a while, and is certainly less threatening than *living* as a conscious person.

---

[22] Tolle, Eckhart. *The Power of Now,* Namaste Publishing, 1997, p. 158.

Often the ego will grant you your "spiritual lifestyle," as long as it emphasizes outer form over inner essence. In fact, the ego is more than happy with all of the spiritual clothing, incense, bells, bowls, CDs, DVDs, and retreats if these potentially useful tools are instead used solely to enhance one's new identity. A spiritual lifestyle may be an improvement over the one we left behind, but it's still a role the ego can happily inhabit since it keeps us at the surface of reality.

Be assured, the deep body awareness that quiets the mind is no more a threat to who we are than a dream. When we wake up from sleeping, the dream story that seemed so real quickly dissolves. When we wake up from the dream of "me," attachment to our personal story disappears just as effortlessly.

Tell me why breathing is one of the practices you emphasize.

Can you feel the expansion and contraction of your torso as you read these words? From the day we are born until the moment of our passing, this part of our body is in motion as a result of respiration.

The majority of the time, *we* don't actually control our breath. Like blinking, cell division, and blood circulation, breathing is mostly a natural bodily process that happens all by itself. However, we do affect the quality of our breathing. Reacting to thoughts and emotions, the body produces breathing patterns that reflect the level of relaxation or distress we are experiencing. Deeper and slower breathing tends to reflect a body and mind that are at ease. Excess physical tension and mental activity are typically accompanied by fast or shallow breathing. This is why people always say to take deep breaths when we are stressed.

Taking slow, deep breaths changes the breathing patterns set by our patterns of thought and emotion. The good news is that there's an open, two-way connection between the mind and the body. Mental patterns affect the body, but the reverse is also true. Changing the body's tension levels and breathing patterns alters our mental and emotional state. Whereas the mind usually affects the physical vehicle by imposing its fear, resistance, and dissatisfaction onto the body, giving our felt attention to the body, including our breathing, reverses the flow, quieting the mind and easing our distress.

Slow, deep breathing can help break up mental and emotional patterns that create pressure and discomfort. An effective deep breath will expand the belly below the navel and produce a longer exhale than inhale. Using this technique means we take temporary control of the natural act of respiration. It can be a great way to start breaking up mind and body patterns before moving on to something more effortless such as simply noticing our breathing. Whether fast or slow, shallow or deep, feeling our breath also frees us from those mental and emotional patterns that abuse the body.

Whether you take control of your breathing or allow it to be as it is, the key is to give it your full and felt attention. Without engaging in a mental commentary, notice the ongoing expansion and contraction of your torso. Feel the sensation of air moving through your nostrils, throat, and lungs without manipulating the natural act of breathing. As you do so, your breathing becomes relaxed, slower, and deeper all by itself.

I'm never sure whether I'm feeling my breath, or whether I just think I am.

Our attempts to use our breathing to become present can easily become a mental activity. We repeat words such as "just breathe" over and over in our head, not really feeling what's happening in the body.

This is why noticing the body's sensations and movements as it performs respiration can be more effective than actively trying to breathe a certain way. We feel our torso moving with every breath, and we feel the air making contact with the inner walls of our nostrils, throat, and lungs. As mentioned earlier, to experience the sensation of air moving through the nose, neck, and chest, it helps to feel the temperature of the air in each inhale and exhale, noticing how our inhales are generally a little cooler than our exhales.

As you breathe just now, can you feel the difference in temperature?

I've never noticed this before. When I feel the temperature of my inhales and exhales, I'm more confident that I'm not just thinking about my breathing.

Yes, and another indication of whether you are feeling your breath is a sense of ease—a sudden reduction of pressure in the body, accompanied by a greater awareness of this moment.

Because the mind has "more important" things to do, the body breathes all day without our noticing it most of the time. Feeling our breath returns us to the reality of the present moment by creating gaps in the thought stream that contains our personal story of lack, want, dissatisfaction, and feeling hurt. Returning frequently to the breath is the path to experiencing peace.

To recap, whenever you remember, take a few minutes to feel the air, usually cooler, moving through your nostrils, throat, and lungs as you inhale. Feel the slightly warmer air in your lungs, throat, and nostrils as you exhale. Feel the movement of your body as it expands and contracts with every breath. Ignore any mental commentary, which in any case becomes quieter and less distracting the longer you inhabit the body and its home, the present moment.

Along with noticing our breath, you talk about unclenching our muscles. But without muscle tension, we wouldn't be able to sit, stand, or do anything.

Without the basic push and pull of atomic forces that create a balanced pressure in the body—for example, intracranial pressure and blood pressure—it's true we couldn't physically exist. However, we don't require the additional tension produced by resisting whatever may be happening at the present moment.

The mind in its egoic state is constantly engaged in some form of resistance, and this resistance produces pressure and tension that builds up in the body throughout the day. Unnecessary bodily tension indicates we are "not here" but are lost in thought. This further dulls our already limited body awareness, pushing us further away from consciousness of the present moment.

One of the most common ways this manifests is in the unconscious clenching of muscles. What purpose does a tight neck or clenched fist serve when we are waiting in line or working at the office? Scan your body right now to see which muscles you have engaged. Are all of these tight muscles necessary as you read or listen to these words?

We can be extra careful when holding a hot dish of food or carrying a fragile package. We can be focused when completing a written proposal and alert when driving to a destination when time is limited. Having a tense jaw or overly tight shoulders is unnecessary tension that serves no purpose in these common scenarios. In fact, this extra tension often makes matters worse, leading to errors and mishaps, as well as psychological and emotional distress.

Throughout your day, notice how much unnecessary tension you carry when working at the computer, driving your car, carrying a hot coffee, or interacting with people. With practice, you'll be able to briefly pause in the middle of an action, unclench your muscles, and complete the activity in a relaxed fashion.

As you learn to unclench and relax, you'll soon realize you can live your busy life with grace and ease. Even hard work can feel effortless when you are relaxed, alert, and only using those muscles necessary to perform a task. A relaxed body results in a quiet mind, since in the absence of strong emotions and physical tension the mind is starved of the fuel it needs to keep thinking compulsively.

I unclenched my jaw and thighs, and I uncurled my toes. I had no idea they were tense. My breathing is a little easier, and I feel more space in my body. But this has brought into focus a background anxiety. I realize much of my tension comes from simply trying to keep my life together. I just want to feel everything is going to be okay.

By observing and feeling your body, you created space for a deeper wisdom to enter and provide you with insight concerning your life.

When we do this, it's not uncommon for negative emotions that have been repressed to rise to the surface.

Allow your emotions to be as they are. As we observed in an earlier chapter, notice that they are essentially energy under pressure. Feel the physical effect of the emotion. Are the sensations moving up and down, left to right, or in circles? Do they feel cool or warm? Does it feel like a tingling or a throbbing, a dull ache, or a sharp pain?

Avoid labeling the sensations as abstract concepts such as fear, betrayal, disappointment, or rage. This keeps the mind engaged and perpetuates the egoic cycle of thoughts producing emotion and physical tension in the body, which in turn act as fuel for yet more incessant thinking.

Energy under pressure requires the confined area of a limited "me" in order to survive. Attention creates space. Negative emotions can't sustain themselves for long in the larger space we create by simply giving the sensations our full attention, free of mental commentary and reactivity. Reducing this excess pressure in the body reduces our resistance to the flow of life.

Since we are heavily identified with what happens in our lives, it's no surprise we go through each day wanting everything to be "okay." Consequently, when we perform our daily chores, we often do so with unnecessary tension that reflects the ego's fear that our lives are falling apart. What we are feeling is the deeper truth that the ego we identify with *is* always on the verge of falling apart.

The false me is under pressure from trying to avoid the misfortune, mistakes, and accidents that threaten its superficial sense of "okayness." Keeping us lost and distracted in the abstract realm of thought is also exhausting, and our attempts to make things "okay" only push us further away from the only place where things are always okay, which is the present moment. Paradoxically, then, while the ego goes through life walking a tight rope, the foundation of reality we walk upon is broad and safe.

Present moment reality is closer to us than our own breath, and no leap of faith from illusory heights is required to enter into it. All we have to do is allow our false "story of me" to unravel. We'll be soothed and reassured by experiencing the peace and goodness we are, as we realize everything has always been and will always be okay.

While feeling the breath alone can relax the body, awareness of our breath becomes more potent when combined with the deliberate unclenching of muscles. It only takes a few seconds to check our jaw, shoulders, and solar plexus and diaphragm—the muscles where the abdomen and ribs meet—and unclench them before we focus on our breathing. These body parts are emphasized because of their location. When clenched, they act as gates that constrict our breathing and the flow of the subtle life force (the body's energy field or chi), limiting our awareness of the heart area.

The heart's power is such that when this region is relaxed, every other part of the body soon follows. As we saw in an earlier chapter, the heart area is an essential gateway through which we become aware we are one with any form and with life itself. It's no accident that the natural life processes of laughing, crying, yawning, and orgasm temporarily create a sense of ease, empathy, oneness, and wellbeing by forcing open these gates and relaxing the heart area. Inhabiting the present moment through deep body awareness accomplishes the same effortlessly and permanently.

Whenever you remember to feel your breathing, check that your jaw, shoulders, and solar plexus-diaphragm region are unclenched. Then focus on your breathing for a minute, scanning your body for any other muscles that need to be relaxed. You may notice tightness in your back and calves. With practice, you'll be able to make your entire body go limp in an instant, leaving only essential muscles engaged.

If I become more relaxed, how will this help me in everyday life?

When we focus on a body part and suddenly notice an aliveness, it appears as if we've created something from nothing. In truth, the sensations are always there waiting to be felt. The more we practice, the easier it becomes to feel what's already and always there. Feeling any sensation at all in a particular body part—warmth, throbbing, prickling, or movement—is helpful for moving our attention back to reality because sensations can only happen *now*. In particular, the more sensitive we become to the subtle energies beneath these surface sensations, the easier it is to perceive the peace that's here but not yet experienced.

Beneath the surface sensations we associate with different limbs and organs, the body can be experienced as a single living energy field. This vital force, sometimes called chi or prana, is a fundamental building block of existence and acts as a bridge between the manifest universe and its unmanifest source.[23]

Anchoring our awareness in the body's energy field is important because the mind in its egoic condition compartmentalizes the natural differences between the various kinds of forms, as if they were separate realities in themselves, instead of simply recognizing the differences and making use of them as required.

Our mental software is designed to label, categorize, and measure forms in order to help us survive and thrive. For instance, we can't get from point A to point B if we can't distinguish between A and B. We also need to know the difference between what's dangerous and what's beneficial—to know that grapes are for eating and bricks for building. The problem is that when the ego is in charge of this software, it takes the differences too far, completely obliterating awareness of their intrinsic oneness. Anchoring our awareness in the body's energy field brings us the balanced perspective of reality we need, so that we are fully aware of the world's separate forms as we simultaneously experience our collective oneness.

Imagine you are watching extreme violence, horror, and sadness unfold before you, but in a movie theater. The reason most people don't become hysterical and have a breakdown is because they know it's just a movie and that they are safe in their seats. Imagine you were unaware of being in a theater. This is the way most people live their lives. Their attention is so completely absorbed by the interplay of forms that they fail to perceive a deeper reality. They are unaware of the body—the theater seat for our true self, so to speak—that could anchor them in reality and keep them at peace.

---

[23] Tolle, Eckhart. *The Power of Now*, Namaste Publishing, 1997, pp. 110-111.

When we feel an aliveness throughout the body, we are more rooted in the here and now. The clarity that emerges makes us aware that the dramas unfolding in our lives aren't exactly as they appear to be. We recognize that at the core of every person, situation, and experience is the universal awareness, wearing its disguises, and that the formless essence of every being remains untarnished and unhurt.

I frequently have trouble sleeping. I also have difficulty waking up when I do finally fall asleep. Can feeling my body help with this?

A good time to cultivate awareness of our "inner energy body"[24] is before falling asleep at night and again upon waking in the morning before we get out of bed.

As we've already seen, all the time we spend waiting during the day gives us ample opportunity to cultivate presence through body awareness. Waiting to fall asleep or waiting to be alert enough to get out of bed and start our day are two of the best times to cultivate present moment awareness. We are already relaxed, or have the intention to relax, and being stationary makes it easier to perceive subtle sensations in the body.

Take your time with the following exercise in order to increase your awareness of your inner landscape. With patience and practice, you'll feel an aliveness throughout your entire body in a matter of seconds and in any situation.

Lying down, close your eyes and let your body sink into the floor or mattress. Let this surface take all your weight. Draw your senses inward and scan your body for unnecessary tension, then unclench your muscles.

Take a minute to feel the temperature of your breathing, then place your attention on your feet. Can you feel them from the inside, so to speak? Can you feel a subtle energetic tingling? Or can you simply feel that they are alive compared to what they are resting on? If you have trouble feeling your feet, you can rub or twitch them, then see if it's easier to feel them.

---

[24] Tolle, Eckhart. *A New Earth*, Dutton, 2005, p. 53.

When you can feel your feet, move your attention to your ankles, then to your shins and calves, knees, thighs, and pelvis. Take time to feel the aliveness in each body part before moving on to the part above it.

At this point, see if you can feel your entire lower body—from pelvis to toes—as a single field of energy.

You may find throughout this exercise that the mind tries to help you by creating mental images of body parts. This will reduce your *felt* awareness and pull you back into abstract mind space. As soon as you notice this happening, drop out of your thoughts and return awareness to *feeling* your body.

Now proceed up your body, feeling your hands, forearms, upper arms, shoulders, and armpits, one at a time. Don't *think* about the body part, just *feel* it. Remember that twitching the muscles in the body part or rubbing it can increase your capacity to feel it in the early stages of your practice. Eventually this won't be necessary. You'll be able to feel a subtle aliveness when you are up and moving around during your day.

Can you feel your abdomen and lower back? Can you feel your chest and shoulder blades? What about your rib cage as it expands and contracts with every breath?

Try to feel the aliveness in your neck before focusing on each part of your head—your jaw, ears, cheeks, lips and tongue, nose and eyes, forehead, crown, and the back of your head.

Complete the exercise by trying to feel your entire body as a single field of energy for as long as you wish.

Can you still feel the aliveness in your body with your eyes open? Shift your awareness from observing your felt aliveness to *being* this aliveness. Bask in the soothing wellbeing that arises from simply feeling alive.

When I feel emotionally overwhelmed, I can't feel the subtle aliveness in my body.

This is another reason feeling our breath and unclenching our muscles is important. Placing all of our attention on relaxing muscles and on the act of respiration can help us quiet even overwhelming emotion. At the very least, it will prepare us to go into the body to experience what's happening there.

Try to experience your emotions as an energy phenomenon under pressure. What are the felt characteristics of this phenomenon? Does it feel dull or sharp, cold or hot? Does the energy move in circles, up and down, or diagonally? Does it feel stuck? Notice that most of this emotional energy exists in your torso.

When you feel emotionally overwhelmed, you can shift your awareness to the periphery of your body. Notice that your toes, elbows, or the back of your knees are largely free of the suffering in the core of your body. Find a body part that isn't suffering and rest your attention there. After a few minutes, see if you can turn your attention back to the center of the emotional energy, observing the sensations with as little judgment and reactivity as possible.

Remember, your nonjudgmental attention creates space, reducing the feeling of emotional trauma by reducing the physical pressure coming from this energy phenomenon. If the emotions are still too strong, you can shift your attention back to the periphery of your body. Periodically moving back and forth from the core of your trauma to the periphery of your body reassures you that *you* aren't the trauma.

The more you practice deep body awareness, the easier it will be to anchor your attention in the body's energy field during good times and bad. It will now be easier to notice that any strong emotional event in the body has finite borders and limited depth.

Many don't need to feel overwhelmed for it to be a struggle to feel their body. Simply being lost in thought makes it difficult. The good news is that the moment we notice we're lost in thought, we're no longer lost in thought! In other words, repeatedly catching ourselves thinking doesn't indicate failure but is rather the stepping stone to success.

Interestingly, it can be difficult to feel the body when we're moving. When we're in motion, the mind becomes fully active, going into autopilot as it assesses, analyzes, and goes over our plans. In the early stages of our practice, or any time we're having difficulty feeling our body, we can focus on the surface sensations of whatever's in contact with our skin.

Can you feel each piece of clothing and each accessory as it makes contact with your body? Can you feel all of this while you move around? Can you feel the impact in your thighs with every step you take?

With practice, you'll be able to shift from the felt experience of surface body sensations to awareness of your subtle energy body. The depth of your body awareness is related to the depth of your present moment awareness. You are on your way to living the whole of your life consciously.

13

THE IMPORTANCE OF THE DAILY AWARENESS ROUTINE AND OTHER PRACTICES FOR EXPERIENCING AND SUSTAINING INNER PEACE

All day, as frequently as possible, return your attention to the here and now. Unclench your jaw, shoulders, solar plexus, and diaphragm.

Drawing your senses inward, feel the sensation of breathing, noticing in your nostrils, throat, and lungs the difference in temperature between your inhales and exhales.

Feel the movement of your torso as it expands and contracts with every breath. Take your time. Your goal is relaxation, not the completion of a technique.

Now move your attention to the sensation of clothing and accessories touching your body. Feel each item, then see if you can feel everything that's touching you all at once. If you're able, go deeper and feel the subtle energetic aliveness within the body.

Your cue to move from one technique to the next is a reduction in the feeling of pressure and unease in the body, or when you find your mind pulling too much of your attention away from your felt experience.

You can cycle through the techniques again to deepen your relaxation. Include the unclenching of muscles throughout your body this time. Don't rush back to your responsibilities and worries, but instead take a few moments to notice the greater sense of ease and wellbeing in your body, and rest your attention there.

Unclenching muscles, experiencing your respiration, and feeling the aliveness throughout your entire body—these three techniques compose your daily awareness routine. This routine forms the basis of all other activities. Whatever you do during the day, use the daily awareness routine to keep yourself relaxed, alert, and as present as possible.

The daily awareness routine can be performed anywhere in as little as thirty seconds without anyone noticing. However, the longer you anchor your attention in the body, the more peace, relief, and freedom you'll feel. In time, the three components of the daily awareness routine are something you'll perform effortlessly as a seamless action.

When learning the daily awareness routine, it's best to be fairly still and have your eyes closed. As you become more familiar with the landscape of your own sensations, you'll have the confidence to deepen your body awareness with your eyes open and your body in motion. At this point you can gradually integrate the daily awareness routine into all your activities.

From responsibilities to pleasures, watch as your entire life becomes a meditation.

The daily awareness routine also forms the basis of any other stress reduction and self-awareness techniques, so that if you have a current favorite technique, its potency is amplified greatly by adding this daily awareness practice.

The mind interprets many common relaxation and awareness efforts as a "doing," causing the body to respond with muscle tension and pressure, which reduce the efficiency of a technique. Because the daily awareness routine is an "undoing," it helps us surrender to the moment and allow everything to be as it is. Returning to the daily awareness routine frequently during the practice of your own techniques counteracts any buildup of psychological and physical resistance.

On its own, the daily awareness routine can dissolve suffering, thereby facilitating the emergence of peace, joy, and clarity. However, different people are drawn to a variety of practices, therefore additional techniques are offered in the following pages and in the various appendices. The practices that have been selected perfectly complement the daily awareness routine and reflect the reality that resistance and suffering manifest differently in each person.

What if I just want to feel my breathing, or maybe just unclench my jaw, throughout the day. Is this good enough?

Your capacity to remain in the here and now will determine what's "good enough." Can you easily return to the present moment by simply feeling your breathing? Are you satisfied with the level of ease and clarity that results? If so, then perhaps this is all you need.

Having said this, you may notice that the depth of your peace and present moment awareness is greater when you include the other components of the daily awareness routine. Together, the three techniques act synergistically, helping us release layers of resistance we wouldn't otherwise be aware of.

You mentioned there are practices that go beyond the daily awareness routine.

Yes, there are. One helpful technique you could try involves simply looking around you. Relax your gaze to focus on the space between you and whatever you're looking at. Feeling your body while you observe empty space, you'll find your attention shifts to the present moment.

You can try this now by noticing the space between you and this page. Feel your focus shift, as if you are noticing a speck of dust floating in front of you. Keep your gaze soft and your face relaxed, otherwise the mind will make use of the tension and resistance to become active again.

Using the daily awareness routine deepens our ability to perceive the space around us. The quiet mind that results allows for a peaceful stillness to emerge. This stillness contains the knowledge and realization that the space outside of us is the same as the vast space within us. As the "me" disappears, perception of the body changes from limited and solid to infinite and spacious. We realize there never was a barrier between inside and outside, "me" and "the other." It was just an illusion.

You look at forms all day, often lost in thought and unaware of what you're looking at. Spending time noticing the space in between you and any form will quiet the mind. What about the space twelve inches in front of that wall or six inches in front of that screen? Can you notice the emptiness halfway between you and the house, tree, or building as you walk or drive around?

You talk about quietness a lot. But I don't like just being quiet. I especially don't enjoy being alone with nothing to do.

Do you find yourself turning on the television or listening to music to keep you company? Or keeping yourself busy with activities that aren't essential? Many are afraid of being alone and having nothing to distract them.

Eleven studies found that participants typically didn't enjoy spending even between six and fifteen minutes in a room by themselves with nothing to do but think. They enjoyed doing mundane external activities much more. The most surprising finding was that "many preferred to administer electric shocks to themselves instead of being left alone with their thoughts." In other words, most would rather be doing something than nothing, "even if that something is negative."[25]

When people are afraid of being alone with their thoughts, the one who's actually afraid is the egoic imposter. The ego dreads silence and being still because noticing external silence promotes internal silence, which leads to the ego's dissolution.

This isn't just about fear, however, but also ignorance. The egoic condition makes us unable to perceive the power of silence. The

---

[25] Timothy D Wilson et al., "Just Think: The Challenges of the Disengaged Mind," *Science,* 4 July 2014, vol. 345, no. 6192: pp. 75-77.

form-based thinker can't fully understand the importance of formless silence, so it looks elsewhere for relief.

Prolonged resistance to the silence of the present moment causes the mind to become increasingly dysfunctional. The voice in the head and its emotional echo in the body become intolerable, which is why people would even prefer to give themselves electric shocks— and why some indulge in masochistic practices such as cutting themselves.

The irony is that this same ego prevents us from seeking the only remedy there is—silent peace. We are left with using external noise and activity in a futile attempt to block out our incessant thinking and emotional reactivity.

You're saying it's really helpful to seek out silence?

To look at empty space is to observe formlessness with our eyes. When we perceive the same formlessness through our ears, it's experienced as silence. When we detect formlessness deep in the body as a feeling, it's experienced as an aware stillness, which can also be perceived outside of us. This peace is our essential being. Space, silence, and stillness are each aspects of the universal awareness as perceived through the different bodily senses.

Reducing the amount of unnecessary noise in your life will make it easier for you to notice the silent witness, your true peaceful nature. Once you recognize it, by feeling it, you'll be able to notice it in noisier situations.

If you're presently in an environment in which there's a certain amount of noise, can you notice the silence between sounds? Can you tune into the silence contained within even the noisiest experience?

Try focusing your attention on the silence just a few inches outside your ears. There may be sounds all around you, but notice there are no sounds originating from the space right next to you.

You may notice that holding your attention on only one aspect of the body, such as your breath, makes it easier for the egoic mind to push its way in and take control of your technique. The moment you notice this happening, unclench your muscles and switch to another point of focus, such as empty space or silence, or bodily sensations. Rotating your attention among these focal points keeps you one step ahead of the ego, which wants all your attention focused on itself.

Our attention is always somewhere. If we currently don't know where our attention is, it's most likely in the abstract realm of thought. The ego, by definition, is the compulsive thinking with which we identify. This means all our attention is typically absorbed by mind activity. Feeling the body and experiencing space, silence, and stillness pulls our attention away from the mind. At first we may only stay in the present for a second or two, as our attention quickly snaps back into the mind. Eventually, we return to our natural state, with our attention at rest in the present.

Throughout the day, ask yourself, "Where's my attention? Where am I? Am I here?" This will shake free your attention and make you more aware of the here and now. Follow this up with the daily awareness routine to deepen your experience of the present. Notice how it's now much easier to perceive space, silence, and stillness.

If alert presence is the key, why can't we bypass the body and simply notice space, silence, and stillness? In other words, why can't we just notice the present moment directly?

As long as we're identified with the mind, we're to some degree identified with our sense perceptions and thus the body. This means that a filter of "me" is superimposed over our looking, listening, and attempts at alertness. Mind identification causes us to be unaware that it's our felt body awareness that's helping us determine what's real and what's illusory. Bypassing a body with which we still identify is the ego's attempt to enter the present moment, which it can never do.

Having said this, what can be bypassed to some degree are the surface sensations of body parts and processes. With practice, we can immediately experience the energy field of the body and the stillness that lies beneath. However, as long as there's the perception of a body, feeling it can't be completely avoided, and even formless awareness will be interpreted as a physical experience of vibrant stillness.

To be anchored in the felt awareness of our body throughout the day is of primary importance. The depth of our awareness is at first limited because we're also focused on performing the daily activities of our lives. This is why it's recommended we also find one or more times during the day when our attention can be completely focused on the experience of our inner landscape. During these sessions, great strides are made in deepening our awareness of the body and the stillness that is our essence.

There are many kinds of meditation, yoga, tai chi, and so on that can help increase the depth of our self-awareness. Our morning and night practice of feeling aliveness in the body is a particularly potent form of meditation. We can extend the length of these sessions by noticing space, silence, stillness, and by adding one or two techniques that can be found in the appendices.

I've been practicing yoga and meditation for years on a consistent basis. I lead a healthy and spiritual lifestyle. What more can I possibly do?

Your practice and beliefs have clearly changed your life in some valuable ways, though from what you've shared, it appears they haven't actually transformed you. If this is the case, it's because the peace, joy, wisdom, and love you seek can't be attained by the seeking "me." In this sense, there's nothing more "you," meaning the ego, can do. The transformation required involves *transcendence* of the false self, not trying to change it.

You may wish to ask yourself the following questions: "What's the quality of my practice? Am I more concerned with maintaining the pose of a Yogi and the demeanor of a Zen monk than I am about what I'm actually experiencing?"

There can be no self-awareness without *feeling* it. Your felt experience is more important than how you look and behave on the outside.

To shift into a feeling state, your body and breath awareness need to expand from brief periods on the yoga mat or meditation cushion to fill your entire day. Otherwise, the ego will find a way to survive and stay in control. The ego is such a master role-player that it tricks people into remaining attached to their personal "story of me," even if the story now includes the quest for peace and awakening.

My meditation practice in particular has reduced my stress, increased my empathy, and opened my eyes to the fact things aren't quite as they appear to be. But I'm beginning to wonder whether a permanent shift in consciousness will ever take place.

The impermanent ego understandably doubts that we will ever awaken to permanent peace because it can never know this experience. Nevertheless, fulfillment and awakening are your destiny, whereas dissolution is the ego's destiny.

Let's assume you meditate twice a day, four to five times a week. That's wonderful. But what about cultivating presence and body awareness during the day? If you're like many, you forget to do it for long periods, since you likely have a pretty hectic life, including children and a demanding job. Being unconscious for most of your day minimizes the chances a shift will take place. A permanent shift in consciousness happens all by itself when the ego is no longer able to impede this natural process. Almost the whole day spent resisting what *is* leaves the ego in control and lessens the chances you'll enter into your peaceful essence.

Unnecessary tension and partial body awareness are an indication the ego is still operating and in control. Sometimes when I meditate with people, I notice they have a slightly furrowed brow. Some also appear to have unnecessary tension in their jaw and shoulders. When I ask them about this, they may describe it this way: "It feels like moving through an empty dark space, and sometimes there are images in my mind's eye. It feels good. I can't say I'm very aware of my body or surroundings, however."

In such a situation, what the person is experiencing is mental journeying, which is just another way for the egoic mind to escape reality. Although temporarily satisfying, it doesn't get them very far.

Traditional awareness practices promote deep concentration and increase our sensitivity to the most subtle forms, such as the breath and chi, and ultimately to formlessness itself. But we can't only cultivate presence in a yoga studio, and body awareness isn't solely for times we sit on the meditation pillow. We must take this deeper felt awareness into the rest of our day, which is the ego's domain.

Once we quiet the mind a little and inhabit our body with our practice, we cease all effort and simply allow everything to be as it is with minimal interpretation or reaction. We remain aware of where our attention is, watching as it naturally shifts its focus between forms and formlessness. We notice that our experience of the present moment, and therefore peace, is deepest when our attention rests on bodily sensations, space, silence, or stillness. If our attention is drawn to thoughts or images, we observe them without attachment by remaining anchored in the body.

Will I always need techniques to become present?

The daily awareness routine moves us from the obvious to the subtle. We begin with the perception of forms and gradually become aware of awareness itself. In other words, the daily awareness routine is a technique that dissolves itself in the act of using it, moving us from effort to effortless being. There comes a point when we cease trying to "be here now" and simply allow everything to be as it is.

We eventually notice that the less we try to manipulate our experience, the deeper our awareness of the present becomes. The more passive form of the daily awareness routine is essentially the cessation of effort, the end of technique. It requires us to do as little as possible. We notice the breathing that's already happening, feel the sensations the body is currently experiencing, watch the body relax all by itself in response to our passive observation of reality.

The ego is the "reality manipulator," and it dissolves as we enter the present, leaving nothing but the experience of what *is*. Reality is experienced, but there's no "me" that's experiencing it.

So who is it who's still passively observing when manipulation has ceased? *We* are—aware stillness, the witnessing presence.

Our eyes open. Perhaps they look around the room. A form is perceived, then another. Attention turns to a sensation in the body. Our eyes close and respiration is felt. The witness becomes aware of a palpable quiet in the room and rests its attention there. All of this happens naturally when the egoic me has disappeared.

The end of technique is the beginning of spontaneous living. Flowing with ease, we allow a higher intelligence to guide our body and mind. We are deeply at rest inside, as life itself takes control of the vehicle.

Being may wish to look at the sky, listen to a bird, or move a leg. When we trust it to take the reins of our practice, we develop confidence it can take the reins of our daily existence.

All of our efforts to cease resisting reality create a significant improvement in the quality of our life. We might liken it to having spent our whole life in a dark, windowless room, and experiencing the outdoors for the very first time—albeit with an overcast sky. But the final step of awakening, the final act of grace, is out of our hands. There's nothing we can do but wait for the clouds to disperse by themselves, revealing the source of this newfound light and warmth.

Our responsibility is to create the conditions necessary to experience the light of pure being. A permanent shift in consciousness can now naturally unfold. Just as surely as the sun emerges from behind the clouds, so the awareness of *You* will emerge from behind the thinker.

CONCLUSION

In 1969, in the city where I was born, John Lennon and Yoko Ono held a Bed-in for Peace. It was there, in Montreal, they co-wrote and recorded what would become an anthem for millions in the years to come, *Give Peace a Chance.*

Imagining peace, calling for peace, and trying to act peacefully are wonderful initiatives that have inspired many. Now we know that a lasting global peace movement can only happen when we notice the actual movement of peace within us and around us. Vibrant peace is always here and has been waiting eons to be experienced and embodied.

Through our attentive presence, it feels as if peace has been "activated" and come to life. From a deeper perspective, it isn't peace that's dormant within us, but we who are asleep to our true peace-filled nature. By fully inhabiting the present moment, we come to life. We awaken and finally give peace a chance to become manifest in ourselves and across the planet.

When we're in a situation where we want something very badly for ourselves or for the world, we often declare under our breath, "Please, I will do anything to make this happen!"

Now, through this teaching, you have the solution. The answer to personal fulfillment and world peace is here, and it's your responsibility. You have it within your means to finally experience what you've always wanted.

If as a species we don't try to return to our true nature, then we and the planet will continue to suffer, and we will have to admit we aren't willing to do anything we can to heal ourselves and the world. In this case, even though we have the *opportunity* for the "story of me" to have a happy ending, the ego is opting for the story of struggle and suffering to go on and on.

"You are peace. Feel your body to end your suffering, and thereby save the world." This is the simple message of this book. The mind finds it hard to believe that such simplicity can be the solution we've longed for, favoring complex, exotic, and esoteric interpretations over what *is*. This is why we need the body, which is always here in the present moment, to help us determine what's real versus what's mind-made fantasy.

Up until now, human beings have failed to appreciate the essential role body awareness plays on the path to peace and awakening. In part, this is unintentional. The seeking ego conceptualizes and therefore distorts the essence of any teaching that leaves much of it open to interpretation. More than a few wars have been waged over competing versions of a spiritual teaching. You may be more interested in ending your stress and suffering than discovering your true nature, but the resolution of both is the same—entering the present moment. However, as we've seen, the truth isn't a concept but a deep knowing based on our felt experience.

The good news is that life doesn't mind how many times you hear this book's message. It will keep repeating it until you embody it. Life is using everything around you and within you to help you wake up. Are you starting to notice? Without an earnest commitment to try for yourself what's been suggested in this book, these words, like so many of life's messages, will become noisy static in the mind.

The egoic mind tries to convince us that life without it would be miserable, whereas the opposite is true. Look carefully at your life and the lives of others. Notice that the person afraid of losing passion is already numb on the sofa and passionless. The person afraid of losing love is already hurting, anxious, and empty on the inside. The person afraid of losing their reputation and influence is already in front of the mirror feeling fake and powerless.

The end of your story means the end of identification with mind content, which brings the end of chronic suffering. This is the beginning of a life lived with true passion, deep peace and love, and a strong feeling of dignity and empowerment.

Peace is the essence of every form we see and saturates every inch of the space around us. This intelligent, vibrant, aware stillness is what we truly are. A life of peace can begin when we no longer take the body for granted. Life itself, on behalf of all of the suffering beings in this universe, awaits our willingness to do so.

Are you ready to play the heroic role you were born to play? The role to end all roles and stories?

Are you ready to be who you truly are?

Appendix I

METTA BHAVANA

Metta Bhavana—metta meditation—is the cultivation of loving-kindness. An ancient practice, it teaches us compassion and how to love unconditionally. The more deeply we feel lovingkindness for all beings, the greater our awareness that all forms are interconnected. This brings us a step closer to the realization that we are one in being.

Metta meditation teaches us what it feels like to have a completely open and surrendered heart. It shows us we are in control of the opening and closing of our heart area. We also realize that our heart is most often in a closed or at least restricted state. This technique can produce the felt realization that we alone are responsible for allowing or blocking what's already here and waiting to be experienced—peace, wisdom, love, and a sense of our collective oneness.

The heart, and the area around the heart, is one of the body's primary portals where the world of forms and its formless source meet. It's through this part of the body that life is most effective in reaching us with its message of awakening and of our collective oneness. It's also where we most easily access universal intelligence and wisdom.

Sitting or lying down, select the following three mental images: someone or something that makes you feel pure love, someone or something for which you feel neutral or indifferent, and someone or something for which you feel great disapproval and dislike.

With your eyes closed, begin with your love image. Visualize it for thirty seconds and notice the effect it has on your body, especially the heart area. Switch to the neutral image and visualize this for thirty seconds. Observe carefully with your felt attention what happens to your heart area. It's likely your chest will feel a little tighter, heavier, or closed. Shift your attention back to the love image and feel how your chest opens up and feels lighter, expansive, and more at ease. You may notice that your breathing becomes a little easier, perhaps accompanied by a relieving sigh. Now visualize your negative image for fifteen seconds, noting the physical changes in your mood and body. How much heavier and tighter is your heart area? Are there any physical sensations similar to emotions? Return to your love image, paying close attention to the felt experience in the body. You can repeat this whole exercise many times during one session. Always finish metta meditation with your love image, basking in the feeling of ease and wellbeing throughout the body for at least three to five minutes.

In the compassion component of metta meditation, we add the following three mental images to the three above: yourself, the world, and the universe. If any of these three were part of your original three images, you will simply have less than six images to work with. Begin with your love image, holding it in your mind for thirty seconds. Proceed to the neutral image, but this time see if you can carry over the relaxed and open feeling in your heart area that your love image produced. Have your loving feelings diminished at all? Go back to your love image and compare the way you heart and body feel now. Your goal is to maintain the same level of love and open-heartedness regardless of the images or thoughts in your mind. Replace your neutral image with each of the following in turn: yourself, the world, and the universe, always returning to the love image for comparison and to relax your body and to fill up on lovingkindness if necessary. Can you maintain the feeling of open-hearted love when you visualize yourself, the world, the universe?

Trying to maintain a relaxed and open heart with feelings of love and compassion may be difficult when visualizing your negative image. This is why we save this exercise for last. You might find that you can only open your heart a little at first. Eventually you'll be able to maintain feelings of love in the face of the most negative image.

***But why should I force myself to love someone who has given me
good reason to dislike them?***

Metta meditation teaches us that compassion for others is really
compassion for ourselves, since there's no completely separate other. A
lot may be happening in your mind with your attention shifting back
and forth between images, thoughts, and reactions. But an outside
observer would see you sitting quietly and alone in your room. No one
is causing you to do anything—you're doing it all to yourself.

Love isn't something that we manufacture for those that we
approve of and deny to those we disapprove of, although it seems
this way. True love is always here and available to be experienced by
anyone who accepts what *is* and can perceive beyond the superficial
level of form. By overreacting to our interpretation of reality, we deny
ourselves the experience of love. This resistance to reality also prevents
us from clearly seeing and understanding the other. You don't have to
like them or approve of them. You just have to stop arguing with reality
so that you can experience the love that you are. The more rooted you
are in your body and the present moment, the more your experience of
love will remain unaffected by whatever appears to be happening out
in the world of form.

Love is more than a feeling. Love is accompanied by the wisdom that
at the deepest level we are a single reality. We begin to see clearly that
those we disapprove of aren't their words and beliefs, and neither are
they the body we perceive. We expect them to believe and behave differently, but their level of consciousness determines what they are able to
understand and how they react. Cultivating lovingkindness reveals that
our interpretation of reality is as distorted and incomplete as theirs,
since we also go through life with a constricted body and a closed heart,
both of which lead to a closed mind. A closed heart not only denies us
of love, but it denies us the wisdom and clarity necessary to understand
reality. With patience and practice you will not require any thought or
image to open your heart, but will be able to do so at will.

Our primary purpose with metta meditation is to realize that
our thoughts, beliefs, and images are largely irrelevant. We have, and

always did have, the ability to keep our heart open or closed anytime we want. We, and no one else, determine whether we will experience the love that we are, the love that's already and always here. If the heart area is open and relaxed, the rest of the body will follow. This means we have deepened our body awareness and thus our awareness of peace.

An additional benefit of having control over the openness of our heart is the immediate dissipation of body urges and cravings. The sense of ease and relaxation produced by an open heart doesn't allow for the buildup of energy in the body that can turn into pressure and cravings for food, sex, drugs, or anything else we engage in with excess. Our body finally receives what it truly craves, which is our unconditional love and attention. Even subtler urges, like the ego's need for security, approval, or control, are significantly reduced. The daily awareness routine by itself can relax the body and heart area in particular. Metta meditation makes the daily awareness routine more potent by teaching us how much control we have over the experience of the heart, the body, and love itself.

Appendix II

TAKE A "YES" WALK

O ur egoic condition makes us resist what is. We are, in essence, saying "no" to reality and are unaware of this. All day we walk around with this unconscious narrative: "No, this is not what I want. I do not approve. I want something else, something more."

By learning to say "yes" to our body and surroundings, we reduce our resistance, thus easing our discomfort and suffering. There is no judgment in our yes, in the sense that we aren't giving our approval or forcing ourselves to like someone or something. Our yes is open-hearted and welcoming, as if we were welcoming loved ones into our home. The tone is, "Yes! I accept life just as it is. I surrender to the wondrous mystery that produced this body and all forms. What a relief that we are one in peace."

In a sense, a yes walk is the mobile version of metta meditation, with both exercises teaching us to approach life with a relaxed body and surrendered heart.

Begin your walk the way you should begin all walks from now on, by feeling all of your clothing and accessories as they contact your body, and by feeling the impact in your thighs with each step you take. Make this your meditation for a few minutes.

Don't walk too quickly, especially in the early stages of your practice. You may notice that the faster you walk, the more mind activity there is. As you look around, softly say yes to your surroundings. Feel the welcoming yes in your body. Feel the relief and pleasurable sensations that emerge from reducing your resistance to reality. Observe your body, your chest in particular, open up and relax as you literally take everything in and accept your surroundings just as they are.

As the scenery changes, say yes again to individual items or the whole scene. Avoid saying yes in rapid-fire fashion to everything you see, since this is the mind taking over an exercise designed to quiet the thinker. Linger in the feelings of lightness and openness before saying yes again.

You use the felt yes to increase the experience of ease and well-being in the body, so this is where most of your attention should remain. What you are saying, as well as what you are looking at, isn't as important as the feelings you are experiencing.

Include your body as one of the items in your surroundings, embracing it with a welcoming yes. Observe as your body releases deep resistance of which you were unaware. Feel the relief and subtle joy as your body opens up like a flower in response to your acceptance and attention.

Use the daily awareness routine periodically to reset your attention and reduce the resistance that builds up from an ego that's trying to perform the exercise "correctly."

Appendix III

THE WITNESSING PRESENCE

B y leaving life alone, allowing everything to be as it is, the egoic "me" disappears. Yet "someone" is still observing what's happening, and this is your true self. The witnessing presence behind all phenomena is always here to observe every experience.

The following exercise helps us become aware of the egoic voice in the head and emotional reactivity—as well as of our true nature, the witnessing presence.

The witnessing presence exercise is performed in two parts. In the first activity, we divide our thoughts into three categories—past, current, and future. We do this exercise with eyes lowered (open and looking down), accompanied by a soft gaze as opposed to a hard stare.

Sitting or lying down, we observe our thought stream and label the thoughts that come to the forefront of our mind. If the thought has to do with something that happened this morning, yesterday, last month, or when we were five years old, we softly say the word "past" and take a conscious breath. If the next thought relates to what's happening currently, we softly say the word "current" and take another slow, deep breath.

Our inner commentary may be expressing something like the following current events: "I'm hungry. Am I doing this right? This is silly. Oh no, I forgot to phone my mother!"

Finally, say the word "future" aloud for any future-oriented thoughts, taking a conscious breath before returning to the activity in your mind. Remember to periodically check your body for unnecessary tension. Unclench any muscles the egoic "me" has engaged, reflecting its efforts to "do" instead of "be."

The reason we vocalize our labeled thoughts is that it helps us stay in the here and now. Observing and labeling our thoughts also helps us feel more empowered vis-à-vis the incessant thinker. We create gaps in our thought stream, proving we continue to exist when thought ceases. This teaches us to take our thoughts less seriously.

Continue this exercise for ten to fifteen minutes and see if you can become more aware of the quiet spaces in between thoughts. The egoic me can't exist for long in these quiet spaces. So who is the one who's aware of these quiet spaces, as well as any thoughts? Your mind can't truly know this answer. Drop out of your thoughts and into your body for the felt experience of the witnessing presence.

The second activity is identical to the first, except we substitute the above labels with the following: thought, emotion, senses. If a thought or mental image is our dominant experience, we softly say the word "thought" aloud and turn our attention to the feeling of our breath. If an emotion in the body grabs our attention, we say the word "emotion" and reset ourselves with a conscious breath. Any physical sensation in the body is labeled "senses." It could be as small as an itch or as large as a headache. Our attention may be drawn to a variety of sense percep-tions, such as external sights, sounds, or smells, as well as the internal sensation of organs or the body's energy field.

These three points of focus—thought, emotion, and senses—encapsulate the normal human experience. Observing our lives in this manner furnishes us with a little distance from the thoughts, emotions, and experiences we take so seriously that they overwhelm us.

Perform this exercise for ten or fifteen minutes. You may notice that the longer you do this exercise, the fewer thoughts and emotions there are to label. Your alert and felt attention quiets the mind, leaving mostly sensations to experience. Unobserved thoughts and unobserved emotions are another way of describing the ego and the pain-body.

The witnessing presence exercise teaches us to look directly at the mind content that runs our life but goes essentially unnoticed. The thoughts and emotions that have such a hold on us lose their potency in the light of our presence.

Appendix IV

QUICK FIXES

I can't concentrate on my breathing when I am moody, frustrated, or impatient. I feel like taking action, like doing something.

Then let's do something. I want you to let your chair take all your weight. Inhale as deeply as you can, then hold your breath. Now clench every muscle in your body, from toes to thighs and fists, including your face. Hold this for a count of four, then exhale through the mouth slowly as you unclench and relax your entire body.

Do this entire sequence—inhaling, holding the breath, clenching, followed by exhaling and relaxing—four more times. You can do this exercise anywhere, sitting or lying down, at home, at the office, or in traffic. It's a good way to calm yourself, as well as a good way to prepare for meditation.

Now, how do you feel?

Better. I feel less pressure in my body.

You built up pressure, then induced muscle fatigue that reduced emotional as well as physical tension in the body. Notice it's not only easier to feel your body, but that the voice of frustration in your head is quieter.

If you now try the daily awareness routine, you'll find it's easier to do. This daily routine takes you deeper into yourself than tensing and relaxing muscles alone.

There's something else you can use as a quick fix. One of the most powerful techniques we can use anywhere is actually a natural body response—yawning. Yawning a few times in a row makes us relaxed, alert, and more empathetic. The connection yawning has to empathy isn't surprising. Yawning—like the natural life processes of laughing, crying, and orgasm—forces the body to relax, breathe deeply, and open the heart area where our connection to the "one life" is most easily felt. Empathy is an indication there's some awareness of our collective oneness, even if it isn't fully understood as such.

Since yawning is an excellent way to reduce pressure in the body, it's a good way to prepare for deeper meditation. It can also help us reduce stress and will instantly boost our energy level. Yawn often throughout the day to refresh yourself, reduce stress, and help yourself shift to a more holistic perspective. You may also find you have access to insights about your situation, or other people even, that your constricted posture and pressured demeanor tend to block. Yawning four or more times in a row increases the potency of this technique. Feel free to stretch your body, since the desire to do so often accompanies a yawn. This also reduces pressure by creating more space. When you've finished yawning, place your attention on your body. Notice it's easier to feel your body from the inside. You can move directly to the daily awareness routine from yawning, since it will deepen your sense of wellbeing.

I don't know how to make myself yawn.

With practice, you'll be able to yawn at will. Many experience an authentic yawn after trying to produce five or six fake yawns. Others yawn successfully by visualizing people or animals yawning. A technique I find effective is to open my mouth by letting my lower jaw slacken and hang down, relaxing my throat, and imagining a tube-like opening pushing air down my windpipe, which fills my lungs up like a balloon.[26]

Some like to use jogging to get into their body and out of their head. Physical exercise, gardening, sex, and so on, can help temporarily. But unlike the daily awareness routine or these quick fixes, we can't perform them all day and when we are engaged in other activities. Even if we combine both quick fixes to help us become more relaxed and alert, they aren't a substitute for the deeper body awareness practices described in this book.

Going back to one of your earlier questions, making body and breath awareness a meditation will make falling asleep on time a little less important. From my experience, one hour of meditation is the equivalent of one to two hours of sleep.

One of the obstacles to falling asleep is the worry that we can't. Turn your attention to your body and breath, knowing that your meditation is just as restful, if not more so, than sleep. This means you no longer have to worry about falling asleep. However, you'll find that the longer you maintain body and breath awareness, the easier it will be to doze off.

---

[26] I learned this last technique from my dear friend and wellness teacher Debra Joy.

 **namaste** **books that change your life**
PUBLISHING

Our Service Territory Expands

Since introducing Eckhart Tolle to the world with The Power of Now in 1997 (followed by Stillness Speaks, A New Earth, and Milton's Secret), NAMASTE PUBLISHING has been committed to bringing forward only the most evolutionary and transformational publications that acknowledge and encourage us to awaken to who we truly are: spiritual beings of inestimable value and creative power.

In our commitment to expand our service purpose—indeed, to redefine it—we have created a unique website that provides a global spiritual gathering place to support and nurture individual and collective evolution in consciousness. You will have access to our publications in a variety of formats: traditional books, eBooks, audiobooks, CDs, and DVDs. Increasingly, our publications are available for instant download.

We invite you to get to know our authors by going to their individual pages on the website. We also invite you to read our blogs: The Compassionate Eye, Consciousness Rising, Conscious Parenting, and Health. Enjoy the wisdom of Bizah, a lovable student of Zen, presented in daily and weekly entries.

We are each in our different ways both teachers and students. For this reason, the Namaste spiritual community provides an opportunity to meet other members of the community, share your insights, update your "spiritual status," and contribute to our online spiritual dictionary.

We also invite you to sign up for our free ezine Namaste Insights, which is packed with cutting edge articles on spirituality, many of them written by leading spiritual teachers. The ezine is only available electronically and is not produced on a set schedule.

What better way to experience the reality and benefits of our oneness than by gathering in spiritual community? Tap into the power of collective consciousness and help us bring about a more loving world.

We request the honor of your presence at
www.namastepublishing.com